THE NEW ZEALAND
VEGETABLE
COOKBOOK

THE NEW ZEALAND VEGETABLE COOKBOOK

LAURAINE JACOBS, GINNY GRANT & KATHY PATERSON

PHOTOGRAPHY BY AARON MCLEAN

RANDOM HOUSE
NEW ZEALAND

CONTENTS

INTRODUCTION

When the three of us set out to write this book with the aim of encouraging readers to cook lots of fresh, wonderful vegetables, two things became very obvious. We wanted to arrange our vegetable recipes by season, and we wanted to keep the recipes simple.

We made endless lists of our favourite recipes, and found that many of our ideas were remarkably similar. So it became an easy process for three authors to share recipes and favourite vegetables and to cook together. And we had so much fun, for working together and sharing kitchen space is very much part of the joy of cooking.

While some of our recipes may seem a little familiar to regular readers of Cuisine and Real magazines, we felt that putting them together in one book, with the addition of lots of new material, would give cooks a resource that they could turn to for enhancing family meals or for entertaining friends.

One of the most significant developments in the culinary scene over the past ten years has been the growth of farmers' markets. Taking shopping bags and filling them with produce that had been growing just a few hours earlier is a real thrill for us. These vegetables connect us to the seasons and rhythms of the earth, and they are so much fresher, crisper and more nutritious than those that have been industrially harvested, transported, distributed, stored and 'supermarketed'. And we love talking to the farmers and getting to know and trust them. All three authors, whenever possible, buy produce daily or no more than a couple of days ahead, and we encourage you to try to do the same.

Many people we know are now planting their own tiny backyard plots, growing veges in tubs on the terraces of apartments, or sometimes embarking on extensive cultivation of well-planned and -tended gardens that take up much of their land. All three authors grow our own herbs and cultivate vegetables to provide fresh food for our tables.

Finally, and significantly, this is not a vegetarian book, but one that celebrates vegetables and vegetable cookery. We're not vegetarians and do not apologise for including the odd mention of meat or fish in our recipes. However, we are certain non-meat eaters will find many recipes to cook in the following pages.

We are all passionate about vegetables and hope to inspire readers to cook different varieties and use the many different ideas and techniques that we have included in this book.

LAURAINE JACOBS, GINNY GRANT AND KATHY PATERSON

SPRING

IN SEASON: Globe Artichokes, Asparagus, Avocados, Beetroot, Broad Beans, Spring Carrots, Fennel, Baby Greens, Baby Leeks, Mint, Peas, New Potatoes, Radishes, Snowpeas, Sorrel, Spring Onions . . .

GLOBE ARTICHOKES WITH ALMONDS AND LEMON

This dish is just as much about textures as flavours. The crunch of the bread and almonds provides a wonderful contrast to the soft artichokes.

4 globe artichokes
3 lemons for preparing artichokes
3 tablespoons olive oil for frying
1 clove garlic, peeled
½ cup day-old bread ground to a coarse crumb
sea salt
zest of 1 lemon and 2 tablespoons juice, for the dressing
3 tablespoons extra virgin olive oil
¼ cup almonds, toasted
2 tablespoons chopped Italian parsley

Use a small knife to peel the artichoke stalks to the pale centre. Snap off the outer leaves of the artichokes so that you are left with the pale hearts. Trim off the tops of the leaves and around the base of the hearts. Cut in half and use a teaspoon to remove the hairy choke from each. Rub all over with the juice of one lemon to stop discolouring, then drop into water that has the juice of one lemon added (acidulated water).

Put in a saucepan with enough salted water to cover the artichokes, and add one cut lemon. Bring to the boil, then simmer gently for 10 minutes or until the artichokes are tender.

While the artichokes are cooking, heat the olive oil in a frying pan. Add the garlic clove and cook until golden. Remove and reserve. Add the breadcrumbs and cook until golden, then remove from the oil and drain them on paper towels.

Make the dressing by mashing the cooked garlic clove with a little sea salt, then mixing with the lemon zest and juice and the extra virgin olive oil.

Drain the cooked artichokes well, discarding the lemon. While the artichokes are still warm, pour the dressing over the top.

To serve, place the artichokes on a platter. Scatter the breadcrumbs, almonds and parsley over the top. Serve immediately.

SERVES 4 AS AN ENTRÉE OR SIDE DISH

MARINATED GLOBE ARTICHOKES

If you are unfamiliar with the preparation and cooking of globe artichokes, this is an excellent way to start. You have probably either tried or seen artichokes in oil, sold in jars. Don't be put off by the amount of olive oil as you can strain off the herbs and garlic, and use the remaining oil and lemon mixture as a vinaigrette. Pure olive oil is fine but extra virgin olive oil achieves an even better flavour.

12 small artichokes (or 6 large)
4 lemons, juice only
1–2 sprigs each marjoram,
    oregano, thyme and parsley
4 fresh bay leaves
2 stalks tender young celery
    with leaves
1 bulb garlic, cloves peeled
salt and freshly ground black pepper
1 litre extra virgin olive oil

Prepare the artichokes: use a small knife to peel the artichoke stalks to the pale centre. Snap off the outer leaves of the artichokes so that you are left with the pale hearts. Trim off the tops of the leaves and around the base of the hearts. Cut in half and use a teaspoon to remove and discard the hairy choke from each. Rub all over with the juice of one lemon.

Blanch the artichokes in boiling salted water for five minutes. Pat dry using paper towels.

Layer the artichokes in a large bowl or jar with the herbs, celery, garlic, salt and pepper. Cover with the olive oil and remaining lemon juice. Marinate for eight hours or overnight.

Serve at room temperature with extra salt available, as this will cut the lemon if you find the vinaigrette a little acidic.

SERVES 6 AS PART OF AN ANTIPASTO PLATTER

Broad Beans, Globe Artichokes, Spring Carrots, Spring Onions And Marjoram

Spring vegetables are simmered in a flavoursome lemon and garlic stock until the artichoke hearts are cooked but the carrots keep a little of their crunch. Delicious to serve with fresh pan-fried fillets of fish, crusty bread and a chilled Sauvignon Blanc.

1kg fresh broad beans
6 large artichokes
3 lemons
¼ cup olive oil
4 cloves garlic, crushed
3 cups vegetable stock
6 small carrots, peeled and cut into even-sized lengths
6 spring onions, trimmed and cut in half on the diagonal
2 teaspoons chopped marjoram
salt and freshly ground black pepper

Remove the broad beans from their pods. Cook the broad beans for one minute in boiling water, drain and refresh under cold water, then remove the skins and discard.

Use a small knife to peel the artichoke stalks to the pale centre. Snap off the outer leaves of the artichokes so that you are left with the pale hearts. Trim off the tops of the leaves and around the base of the hearts. Cut in half and use a teaspoon to remove and discard the hairy choke from each. Rub all over with the juice of one lemon to stop discolouring, then drop into water that has the juice of one lemon added (acidulated water).

Cut the artichoke hearts into quarters and place in a saucepan with the juice of the remaining lemon, the olive oil, garlic and stock. Bring to the boil, then reduce the heat and allow to simmer for 10 minutes.

Add the carrots, spring onions and half the marjoram, salt and pepper. Continue to simmer for 10 minutes.

Add the broad beans and simmer for a further two minutes. Taste for seasoning, then add the remaining marjoram. Place the vegetables and cooking juices in a shallow bowl or platter. Serve warm.

Serves 6 as a side dish or in a shared meal

CREAMY ASPARAGUS SOUP

A rich, creamy soup with a dominant asparagus flavour, boosted with onion, leek and potato. Use chicken or vegetable stock and finish it with crème fraîche and chopped parsley. Accompany with crisp wholemeal toast and a glass of dry sherry.

1kg asparagus spears
1 litre chicken or vegetable stock
3–4 sprigs thyme
2 tablespoons olive oil
2 onions, finely chopped
1 leek, finely chopped
3 large potatoes, peeled and diced
150ml cream or crème fraîche
salt and freshly ground black pepper
parsley sprigs, chopped

Snap or cut the tough ends from each asparagus spear. Bring the stock to a simmer and add these ends and the thyme sprigs. Simmer for about 25 minutes to extract maximum flavour from the asparagus. Strain into a bowl and discard the asparagus ends.

Meanwhile, heat the oil in another saucepan and add the onions, leek and potatoes. Stir to coat in the oil, then add a little water and cook very gently until the vegetables are very soft and well cooked. Add the strained stock and simmer a few minutes longer.

Chop the asparagus roughly, reserving the tips for garnishing. Add the chopped asparagus to the pan with the vegetables and stock and simmer for just five minutes. Any longer and you risk losing the lovely green colour.

Immediately purée this mixture in a blender, then pass through a sieve to ensure no stalky fibres remain in the soup.

To prepare the tips, cut each in half lengthwise and boil in salted water for about two minutes.

To serve, reheat the soup to simmering point. Heat the cream in a small pan, stir into the soup carefully and season to taste with salt and pepper. Ladle into bowls and garnish with the reserved asparagus tips and chopped parsley.

SERVES 6 AS A STARTER

Grilled Asparagus with Anchovies And Lemons

Grilling asparagus brings out a lovely nutty flavour. This platter of chargrilled asparagus, dressed with a paste made with sautéed anchovies, olive oil, lemon and Italian parsley, can be served with flat bread as a starter or luncheon dish. Accompany with a light red such as a Grenache.

750g fresh asparagus spears
8 tablespoons (120 ml) extra virgin
   olive oil
salt and freshly ground black pepper
1 red onion, finely chopped
1 tin (approximately 50g) anchovy
   fillets, drained and chopped —
   we used Ortiz
1 lemon, zest and juice
4 tablespoons finely chopped
   Italian parsley

Heat a ridged grill pan or a barbecue grill until almost smoking. Trim the woody ends off the asparagus spears. Rub the spears with half the olive oil, and scatter salt and pepper over them. Place the spears on the hot grill and cook, turning frequently and watching carefully to ensure they do not burn. The asparagus should grill for seven to eight minutes, until it is tender and has light 'stripes' from contact with the grill.

Meanwhile heat a small heavy-based frying pan, place the remaining olive oil with the chopped onion and cook until soft. Lower the heat, add the anchovies and stir, cooking very slowly with the lemon zest until the anchovies are almost melting. Stir in the lemon juice, add the parsley and adjust the seasoning if necessary. Spoon this sauce over the asparagus and serve at once with flat bread.

Serves 6 as a starter

Mozzarella, Cucumber and Asparagus

The simplicity of flavours is what makes this dish stand out. We used chives in the dressing, but fresh chervil would work well here too. Serve with a crisp Sauvignon Blanc and, if serving for lunch, with crusty bread.

250g buffalo mozzarella
24–30 asparagus spears
2 tablespoons finely chopped chives
3 tablespoons extra virgin olive oil
1 tablespoon lemon juice
½ cucumber, peeled and thinly sliced
sea salt and freshly ground black pepper

Slice the mozzarella, then cut each slice into quarters. Set aside.

Cut or snap off the base of each asparagus spear, peel the lower stalks if woody then slice each in half on a diagonal. Blanch for one minute in boiling salted water then plunge into cold water, drain and dry well.

Mix together the chives, oil and lemon juice. Toss the asparagus and cucumber with half this dressing, then place on plates. Place a few pieces of mozzarella on each plate, drizzle with the remaining dressing and season with salt and pepper.

The asparagus, cucumber and dressing can be prepared ahead of time if need be, but once the salad is dressed it should be eaten immediately.

SERVES 6 AS AN ENTRÉE OR A LIGHT LUNCH DISH

Asparagus Wrapped in Herb Omelettes with Lemon Vinaigrette

Playing on the classic asparagus served with a poached egg, this makes a great brunch dish served warm or cold on a picnic. Slightly under-cook the omelettes, as the egg will continue to cook after being removed from the heat.

18 large green asparagus spears
6 tablespoons extra virgin olive oil
3 tablespoons lemon juice
½ teaspoon Dijon mustard
salt and freshly ground black pepper

For the omelettes
6 eggs
1 tablespoon milk
1 tablespoon finely chopped herbs (we
    used mint, parsley and lemon thyme)
2 tablespoons grated Parmigiano
    Reggiano
salt and freshly ground black pepper
olive oil for omelette pan

Remove the woody ends of the asparagus spears and discard. Blanch the asparagus in boiling salted water for two to three minutes until just tender, then drain.

To make the vinaigrette, place the extra virgin oil, lemon juice, mustard, salt and pepper in a screw-top jar. Shake well, and again just before using.

To make the omelettes, place the eggs, milk, herbs and cheese in a measuring jug and whisk lightly using a fork. Season well with salt and pepper.

Heat the pan to a medium to high heat and lightly coat with olive oil. Pour a one-egg portion into the pan, tilting it so it covers the base. Using a small palette knife, start to draw the edge of the omelette into the middle so the liquid egg runs into the space, continuing until almost all the liquid egg is cooked. Flip the omelette if necessary to finish cooking the liquid egg. Remove from the pan and continue cooking with the remaining mixture to make six thin omelettes.

Wrap three asparagus spears in each omelette, place on six serving plates and drizzle each with a tablespoon of vinaigrette.

Serves 6 as a brunch dish

Asparagus and Three-Cheese Tart

Asparagus combines beautifully with cheese. Serve this tart with a crisp pastry crust filled with asparagus tips, ricotta, Parmigiano Reggiano and feta for a lovely luncheon idea. Perfect with a crisp Sauvignon Blanc and a green salad.

For the pastry case

200g flour
130g butter, ice cold and diced
25g Parmigiano Reggiano, very
  finely grated
3 tablespoons ice-cold water

For the filling

350g asparagus spears, cut into
  3–4cm lengths
200g fresh white cheese such as
  labne or ricotta
4 eggs
a grating of nutmeg
salt and freshly ground black pepper
25g Parmigiano Reggiano, grated
150g crumbly feta

Preheat the oven to 180°C.

To make the pastry, place the flour, butter and Parmigiano Reggiano in a food processor and pulse together until the mixture resembles fine crumbs. Pour the ice-cold water through the feed tube, with the motor running, until the crumbs moisten and start to draw together (this will take only a few seconds). Turn the pastry out onto a clean bench and knead it to ensure it is smooth. Roll out in a circle to fit a 24cm loose-bottomed flan tin. Place it in the tin and trim the edges neatly.

Crush a large piece of baking paper to soften so you can push it right into the corners, and then spread it out across the pastry case. Fill with baking beans and bake blind for 15 minutes until the pastry is a very light sand colour. Leaving the temperature at 180°C, remove the baked case from the oven. Cool slightly.

To make the filling, blanch the asparagus in simmering salted water for two or three minutes, and immediately plunge into cold water to retain the fresh green colour.

In a bowl, beat the labne or other fresh white cheese with the eggs, nutmeg, salt and pepper until smooth.

Grate the Parmigiano Reggiano over the base of the baked pastry case. Crumble half the feta over this, then pour the white cheese and egg mixture in. Lay the asparagus pieces on top of this mixture, and finally top with the remaining feta.

Return the pie to the heated oven and bake for 30 minutes, until the mixture starts to turn golden. Allow to stand a few minutes before serving with a fresh green salad.

Serves 6–8 as a main course

SPRING MEANS . . . ASPARAGUS

Asparagus is our favourite spring vegetable and we all eagerly await the very
first bunches to appear in the markets. They always seem to be quite the sweetest
of the season.

ALL ABOUT ASPARAGUS

You may be lucky enough to find three colours of asparagus: green, purple and white. Green is
the most common variety and has the classic herbal grassy flavour. The purple variety tends to
be sweeter, but it will turn an olive green colour when it is cooked for more than one minute.
The white asparagus that is highly prized in Europe can sometimes be found; it tends to have a
more delicate flavour.

When you're buying asparagus, try to choose spears that have tightly closed tips, rather than
tips that have opened up and look more flower-like. They should be moist and firm.

To get the best out of your fresh asparagus (and it is at its most delicious the day it is picked),
either: recut the stalky ends and stand the spears in water, or place the asparagus in a sealed
plastic container. Store it in the refrigerator until needed.

Cook stores sell special upright asparagus steamers. They are fine as the tips do not get
damaged, but as the most heat from boiling water comes from the actual steam, the spears may
just as well be cooked in a large wide pan where you can watch them carefully and gently lift
them out.

The best wine matches for asparagus are aromatic white wines: Riesling, Gewürztraminer and
very fruity Sauvignon Blanc.

SNAP, PEEL, CHOP?

There's often discussion among cooks about whether or not to peel asparagus. We recommend
that you peel asparagus, as the skin on the lower part of the stalk can be quite tough.
Removing it makes each spear very tender from the tip to the end.

Some people prefer thick asparagus spears as there's more left after the spears are peeled, but
thick and thin are equally delicious.

Later in the season, asparagus often catches dirt in the little nodes on the sides of the stalk.
You can soak them carefully so the dirt floats off, but that is when peeling really comes into its
own, as the spears can be washed again once they're peeled.

When preparing asparagus, many cooks suggest you snap off the stalky end. However,
sometimes a few centimetres are wasted when you do this as the spear will snap wherever you
put the pressure on. An alternative is to look at the asparagus, decide just where it gets tough
and chop it neatly at that point.

ASPARAGUS TIPS

- A large platter of bright green asparagus can be dressed with the following or presented as a cocktail dish with the accompaniment beside it in a dipping bowl:

    - melted butter
    - hollandaise sauce
    - beurre blanc sauce
    - lemony mayonnaise
    - chopped hard-boiled egg and parsley
    - soft coddled egg and black pepper
    - lemon-scented extra virgin olive oil
    - orange segments and chopped pitted olives
    - breadcrumbs cooked in butter or oil with added mustard powder
    - melted raclette cheese
    - crumbled goat's feta

- Wrap blanched asparagus spears in prosciutto or bacon and pop under the grill for a few minutes.

- Make the classic asparagus rolls with the freshest of sliced white bread, fresh lemon mayonnaise and blanched fresh asparagus.

- Roll blanched asparagus spears in finely sliced ham that's lightly spread with Dijon mustard and secured with toothpicks.

- Spread thin slices of smoked salmon with crème fraîche and roll these around asparagus spears for a cocktail idea.

- For an artistic vegetable serving idea, tie bundles of five or six asparagus spears together with the fresh green leaves of spring onions.

BLANCHING VEGETABLES

Vegetables are often blanched before being added to a stir-fry, or for a salad. Stir-frying is a quick process and the softer ingredients like mushrooms or spinach can get mushy while other firmer vegetables like carrots and cauliflower require a longer cooking time. By plunging the firmer crisp vegetables into rapidly simmering salted water for two or three minutes, you partially cook them. Then everything can be combined and cooked for minimal time to complete the recipe.

With green vegetables like asparagus, broccoli and beans, it's important to plunge the blanched vegetables immediately into ice-cold water to stop the cooking process and retain the bright green colour.

BABY COS SALAD WITH AVOCADO DRESSING

This simple green salad is fantastic when Hass avocados are at their best, in late spring. It is best to use the vibrantly coloured dressing as soon as possible — it will soon discolour.

FOR THE DRESSING

1 avocado, preferably Hass
1 clove garlic, peeled
2 tablespoons extra virgin olive oil
   (or avocado oil)
2 tablespoons lemon juice
3 tablespoons crème fraîche
a few drops Kaitaia Fire or
   Tabasco sauce
sea salt

FOR THE SALAD

4 tablespoons olive oil
2 slices day-old sourdough or
   ciabatta bread, cut into cubes
sea salt
1 baby cos, leaves separated
1 spring onion, finely chopped
2 tablespoons finely chopped chives

To prepare the dressing, combine all the ingredients in a food processor until smooth. This makes approximately one cup of dressing.

For the salad, heat the olive oil in a frying pan and toast the bread until golden. Drain on paper towels and season with sea salt.

When ready to serve, place the baby cos, spring onion, chives and half the avocado dressing in a bowl and toss together. Add more dressing if necessary and check the seasoning. Place in a serving dish and scatter the croutons over the top.

SERVES 4 AS AN ENTRÉE

Guacamole

Traditionally this much-loved dip is made in front of guests, using a molcajete (the Mexican version of a mortar and pestle) and eaten immediately. You can use a food processor, but keep the dip chunky. Placing the avocado stones with the guacamole in its serving bowl helps prevent discolouring. Serve as a dip with crudités and corn chips.

3 tablespoons finely chopped red onion
   or shallots
1 red chilli (or to taste), seeded
2 tablespoons coriander leaves
½ teaspoon salt
3 large avocados, halved, stoned
   and peeled
1 cup diced fresh tomato

For the topping
1 tablespoon finely chopped red onion
   or shallot
1 tablespoon chopped coriander leaves
2 tablespoons diced fresh tomato

Using a small food processor, process the onion, chilli, coriander and salt to a rough paste.

Mash the avocados roughly, then stir in the onion mixture and diced tomato. Place in a serving bowl and sprinkle the topping ingredients over the top of the guacamole.

Serve immediately or, if serving later, cover tightly, pressing plastic wrap on to the surface to prevent browning.

Serves 6 as a starter

Oven-Roasted Beetroot with Melted Butter, Parmesan and Herbs

A simple recipe where the beetroot is definitely the star. Roasting the beetroot in the oven in its own leaves produces a flavour that is concentrated and sweet, quite different from beetroot boiled in water. We love the flavour of melted butter, but you could use extra virgin olive oil or a red wine vinaigrette. Serve as a starter or as a vegetable dish with spring lamb and a glass of Pinot Noir.

1kg beetroot, all of a similar size,
   leaves reserved
100g butter, melted
salt and freshly ground black pepper
Parmigiano Reggiano
1 tablespoon roughly chopped Italian
   parsley or snipped chives

Preheat the oven to 180°C.

Place the beets in a shallow roasting dish and cover with their own leaves. Roast beets for about an hour and a quarter, until the skins start to wrinkle and will slip off easily, and the beets are soft when a sharp knife is inserted. Peel and slice evenly while still warm and divide between six serving plates. Pour the melted butter over the beets, sprinkle with salt and grind plenty of black pepper on top.

To serve, shave Parmigiano Reggiano over the whole and finish with a sprinkling of parsley or chives.

SERVES 6 AS A STARTER OR IN A SHARED MEAL

Baby Beetroot, Green Bean and Goat's Cheese Salad with Tangelo Dressing

This salad is easy to put together. Pour the dressing over the beetroot while it is still warm so it gets the chance to soak up the flavours. If tangelos are unavailable use orange juice for the dressing.

For the dressing
3 tablespoons tangelo juice
2 tablespoons extra virgin olive oil
1 teapoon Dijon mustard
sea salt

For the salad
300g baby beetroot, leaves removed and
  reserved
250g green beans, topped and tailed
50g goat's feta or chèvre, crumbled

To prepare the dressing, mix together all the ingredients and set aside.

Cook the beetroot in salted water for 15 to 20 minutes or until tender. When they are cool enough to handle, remove and discard the skins. Slice each in half, then pour the dressing over the beets. Blanch the leaves for two to three minutes until tender, drain and set aside.

Blanch the beans for three to four minutes in boiling water until tender. Drain and refresh in cold water. Drain again and dry with a clean tea towel.

When ready to serve, toss the beans and beetroot leaves with the beetroot and place on a platter. Add the crumbled cheese and serve.

Serves 4–6 as a side dish

BROAD BEAN AND ASPARAGUS SALAD

Toss the broad beans, asparagus and mint with the vinaigrette just before serving so you keep the vibrant green colour of the spring vegetables. Alternatively, you can cook the asparagus on a barbecue grill until lightly charred and bite-tender. Perfect as a vegetable salad with lamb cutlets and new season's potatoes.

500g broad beans
18 asparagus spears
1 teaspoon Dijon mustard
6 tablespoons olive oil
2 tablespoons wine vinegar
salt and freshly ground black pepper
4 sprigs fresh mint

Pod the broad beans and place in a saucepan of boiling salted water. Boil rapidly for two minutes, then drain and refresh under cold water. Remove the outer grey skin and discard, leaving only the bright green beans.

Remove and discard the woody ends of the asparagus spears. Cut the spears in half crosswise and blanch in boiling salted water for two minutes, or until just tender. Place the broad beans and asparagus on paper towels to drain well.

Whisk the mustard, oil and vinegar together and season with salt and pepper. Remove the leaves from the mint sprigs and slice finely.

Toss the broad beans, asparagus and mint together, moisten with the vinaigrette and serve at room temperature.

SERVES 6 AS A SIDE DISH

Broad Bean and Fennel Sauté with Summer Savory

Summer savory is a classic accompaniment for beans but has fallen out of favour in recent years. This annual has a strong flavour with aniseed notes that mellow during cooking (winter savory is a coarser, more bitter-tasting perennial). Vegetable shops or supermarkets seldom stock it: get it from plant stores or seed companies.

The pods of broad beans are too tough to eat unless they are smaller than your little finger. The grey-green skins of the beans themselves tend towards bitterness, so are often removed before cooking. This is sometimes called double podding.

Try this dish on bruschetta as a starter or as a side for grilled fish.

2 large bulbs fennel, fronds reserved
1 tablespoon extra virgin olive oil
1 tablespoon summer savory, chopped
2 cloves garlic, peeled and sliced
500g broad beans (double podded to
   give approx 2 cups beans)
4 tablespoons crème fraîche
sea salt
lemon juice

Remove and discard the outer leaves of the fennel. Cut the bulbs in half and slice thinly. In a medium-sized saucepan, heat the olive oil and gently sauté the fennel for a few minutes until tender.

Add half the summer savory and all the garlic and sauté for another minute. Add the broad beans and crème fraîche and cook for a few minutes until the broad beans are just tender. Meanwhile, chop the reserved fennel fronds.

Season with salt, add the remaining summer savory and chopped fennel fronds and lemon juice to taste.

SERVES 4 AS A SIDE DISH

Fennel, Rocket, Apple and Mint Salad

This salad is designed to whet the appetite. Serve a small pile to each person and hand around thin, crunchy toast to complement the leafy vegetables. Perfect with crusty bread and a fragrant medium dry Riesling.

2 red-skinned apples
1 lemon, juice only
2 cups baby rocket leaves
2 small bulbs fennel, trimmed
   and finely sliced
6 baby beetroot, cooked and cut
   into wedges
1 cup mint leaves, finely sliced
¼ cup medium dry Riesling
¼ cup grapeseed oil
2 teaspoons Dijon mustard
salt and freshly ground black pepper
6 thin slices white bread
extra oil for brushing
½ cup tiny cubes of firm feta

Preheat the oven to 180°C.

Core the apples and finely slice. Immediately cover them with the lemon juice to prevent them turning brown. Take special care to coat them entirely if you are preparing the apple in advance.

Place the rocket leaves in a large bowl. Add the sliced fennel, beetroot wedges, apple slices and half the mint. Toss well together.

Make a vinaigrette by shaking the wine, oil, mustard and plenty of salt and pepper together in a jar.

Meanwhile, cut the crusts from the bread, and cut each slice into three fingers. Brush the fingers lightly with the oil and bake for about 10 minutes until golden and crunchy.

The recipe to this point can be prepared two or three hours ahead. If preparing the toast ahead, store it in an airtight container.

Add the feta to the salad. Toss with the dressing immediately before serving.

Divide the salad between six plates and scatter the remaining mint over each serving. Hand around the toast and serve with a glass of chilled Riesling.

SERVES 6 AS A STARTER OR A LIGHT LUNCH DISH

Shaved Fennel, Radish and Pasta Salad Dressed with Mint and Pink Peppercorns

Fresh and light, this recipe can be prepared with a minimum of effort if you have a Japanese mandolin for the slicing. Otherwise, the slicing blade on a food processor will work, or you can try slicing with a very sharp knife, but the slices of fennel and radish will tend to be a little thicker.

1 cup small pasta shapes (cavatelli, little bows or similar)
8 tablespoons (120ml) extra virgin olive oil
2 medium-sized bulbs fennel, trimmed
6 radishes
1 large avocado
1 cup mint leaves
2 teaspoons pink peppercorns
2 limes, juice and zest
salt and freshly ground black pepper
1 tablespoon Dijon mustard

To make the salad, simmer the pasta shapes in a large pan of well-salted water until tender, but still al dente. Drain well and toss with two tablespoons of the olive oil so the pasta does not stick together. Allow to cool.

Remove the leafy tops from the fennel and discard. Slice the fennel bulbs and radishes with a mandolin so they are paper thin. Peel the avocado and chop it into chunks. Place the mint leaves in a serving bowl with the sliced radishes and fennel, the avocado and the cooked pasta.

Make a dressing by mixing the pink peppercorns, lime juice and zest, the remaining olive oil, salt, pepper and mustard. Toss this over the salad, folding carefully.

Serves 6 as an entrée or in a shared meal

Gingered Baby Carrots and Snowpeas in a Cumin Glaze

A lovely, simple way to add flavour to carrots. Prepare the vegetables ahead then toss in a buttery glaze to accompany steamed rice or noodles.

20–24 baby spring carrots, scrubbed
4cm thumb of ginger, peeled
  and grated
salt and freshly ground black pepper
400g snowpeas, topped and sliced in
  half lengthwise
30g butter
1 teaspoon cumin seeds

Place the carrots in a steamer with half the grated ginger and a little salt. Steam for 10 minutes, until tender. About five minutes into the process add the peas on top of the carrots, with the rest of the ginger. If there is not enough room in the steamer, steam the peas separately.

Turn the steamed vegetables out on to a heated serving platter, adding a few grinds of pepper. Melt the butter in a small saucepan and add the cumin seeds. Tip this mixture over the vegetables and serve at once.

Serves 4–6 to accompany a main course

SPRING VEGETABLE GREEN CURRY

The subtle herbs and spices of Thai-style green curry are perfect for a spring vegetable meal. The recipe calls for a variety of the spring harvest, so feel free to add or substitute other treats from the garden when they're ready to pick.

4 small bulbs fennel
1kg baby new potatoes
2 tablespoons vegetable oil
  (canola or safflower)
2 tablespoons Thai green curry paste
200g baby spring carrots, scrubbed
4 firm but ripe tomatoes, peeled
  and quartered
500ml water or vegetable stock
300g snow beans or string beans,
  trimmed
500g baby spinach leaves
½ cup coconut cream
salt and freshly ground black pepper
½ cup coriander leaves, finely chopped

Trim the fennel bulbs and cut into quarters lengthwise. Scrub the potatoes and cut them into halves. Heat a large wide heavy pan, add the oil and when it is hot, tip in the fennel and potatoes. Stir well to coat with oil and then add the curry paste. Continue stirring so the aromas of the curry are released. Add the carrots, tomatoes and water or stock and bring all to a simmer, stirring well.

Place the lid on the pan and allow the vegetables to simmer gently until the potatoes are tender. This should take 15 to 20 minutes. The curry can be prepared ahead to this point.

Add the beans and spinach with the coconut cream and simmer a further five minutes. Add salt and pepper to taste.

Finally, add the coriander. Serve with steamed rice and a little of your favourite mango chutney.

SERVES 4–6 AS A MAIN COURSE

Braised Spring Vegetables

This simple treatment for spring vegetables is a great dish to adapt with whatever vegetables are available. Add artichokes and asparagus while they are in season. Frozen broad beans and peas are fine to use here if you must.

2 bulbs fennel, fronds reserved
2 tablespoons olive oil
1 leek (white part only), thinly sliced
small bunch baby carrots, scrubbed
½ cup dry white wine
½ cup chicken or vegetable stock
250g broad beans, podded and peeled
100g sugar snap peas
½ cup peas
¼ cup mint leaves, finely sliced
sea salt

Remove and discard the outer leaves and core of the fennel bulbs, then cut the remainder into six pieces. Chop the fronds and set aside. In a medium-sized saucepan, heat the oil and add the leek and fennel pieces. Cook over gentle heat, stirring occasionally, for about 10 minutes — until soft.

Add the carrots, wine and stock, cover and gently simmer for 10 minutes. Add the broad beans, sugar snaps and peas, cooking for another three minutes or until the greens are tender. Add the mint and chopped fennel fronds, then season with salt.

SERVES 6 AS A SIDE DISH

Green Garlic, Leek, Pea and Fresh Herb Risotto

Green garlic is one of the delights of spring, but it is not easy to find unless you shop at farmers' markets, have an Asian green grocer or your own vegetable garden. This recipe would also work well with broad beans.

1.5 litres vegetable or chicken stock

4 tablespoons butter

1 onion, finely chopped

small bunch green garlic shoots, roughly chopped

1 leek, finely sliced

2 cups Arborio rice

salt and freshly ground black pepper

200ml dry white wine

1 cup green peas, fresh or frozen, blanched

¼ cup grated Parmigiano Reggiano

1 cup chopped herbs (parsley, basil, chives, etc.)

extra grated Parmigiano Reggiano for serving

Heat the stock in a large, heavy-based pan and keep at a low simmer. In a similar pan, melt the butter then add the onion, garlic and leek. Cook over a gentle heat until soft and translucent, about five minutes. Add the rice with a pinch of salt and cook over low heat for three minutes, stirring often. Turn up the heat and pour in the white wine, stirring well. When the wine has been absorbed, ladle in enough hot stock to cover the rice, stir well and reduce the heat.

Keep the rice at a gentle simmer and keep adding stock, allowing it to be absorbed into the rice before you ladle in more. After about 10 minutes the rice will be softened but will still be hard in the centre. Stir in the peas and continue to ladle in the stock. After five more minutes, the rice should be completely softened and saucy but not gluey.

Stir the cheese through with the herbs, and season with salt and pepper. Serve at once with extra cheese.

Serves 4 as a main course

WARM ROASTED LEEK SALAD

Prepare this salad ahead and gently warm just before serving. It has a very citrusy dressing of orange and lemon, and would be lovely served with a Riesling.

30 baby leeks
2 tablespoons olive oil
salt and freshly ground black pepper
100g snowpeas
½ cup peas, fresh or frozen
2 oranges
3 tablespoons lemon juice
3 tablespoons extra virgin olive oil
3 tablespoons pitted olives, finely chopped
1 cup chervil or parsley leaves

Preheat the oven to 180°C. Trim the leeks neatly, leaving them whole. In a roasting pan, toss them in the oil and sprinkle with salt and pepper. Roast for 15 to 20 minutes, until they are tender and sweet.

Meanwhile, top the snowpeas and cut them into thin strips. Blanch for one minute in boiling salted water, remove with a slotted spoon and plunge immediately into cold water to retain the fresh green colour. Simmer the peas until tender in the salted water, then drain and refresh these too.

To make the dressing, peel the oranges with a knife, taking care to remove all the skin and pith, and cut into neat segments. Put the lemon juice in a bowl, add salt and pepper and whisk in the olive oil. Add the finely chopped olives with the orange segments, taste and adjust the seasoning if necessary.

To serve, place four or five leeks on each plate, then arrange the snowpeas and peas casually over the top. Divide the herbs between the plates, and finally spoon the orange dressing over each serving.

SERVES 6 AS A STARTER OR LIGHT LUNCH DISH

MEYER LEMON RISOTTO

The sweet flavour and low acidity of Meyer lemons, along with their excellent skin and high juice content, make them a favourite lemon variety (having a reasonably prolific tree helps too). Here they make a rich yet tart risotto that is delicious by itself but also good with seafood.

Ferron rice is the only risotto rice that can be used for the non-stir method on the following page, so if you are using another type, follow the traditional stirring method.

2 Meyer lemons
20g butter
1 tablespoon olive oil
1 onion, finely chopped
2 cups chicken or vegetable stock,
  more if needed
1 cup vialone nano, carnaroli,
  Arborio or Ferron rice
½ cup dry white wine
¼ cup cream
30g Parmigiano Reggiano, grated
1 teaspoon sea salt, approximately

Grate the zest of the lemons and set aside. Remove the skin and pith from the lemons and use a small paring knife to remove the lemon segments. Squeeze any remaining juice over the segments and set aside.

STIR METHOD

Heat the butter and olive oil in a wide saucepan, add the onion and fry gently until soft but not coloured (around 10 minutes). Meanwhile, in a separate pan, heat the stock until hot. Add the rice and half the lemon zest to the onion, stir and coat with the oil and fry for a few minutes, then add the wine and stir until all the liquid has evaporated.

Add the hot chicken stock a ladleful at a time, stirring constantly until all the liquid is absorbed before you add the next ladleful. The risotto should be kept at a rapid simmer. Continue, a ladle at a time, until the rice is al dente (around 20 minutes, but start checking after 15 minutes).

Add the remaining lemon zest, the cream and Parmigiano Reggiano and stir well. Season with salt to taste. Set aside for a minute to allow the flavours to infuse, then add the lemon segments and any juice just before serving.

SERVES 4 AS AN ENTRÉE

(SEE PAGE 46 FOR NO-STIR METHOD)

MEYER LEMON RISOTTO (CONTINUED FROM PAGE 44)

NO-STIR METHOD

Use this method only with Ferron rice. Heat the butter and olive oil in a wide saucepan, add the onion and fry until soft but not coloured (around 10 minutes). Meanwhile, in a separate pan, heat the stock until hot. Add the rice and half the lemon zest to the onion, stir to coat with the oil and fry for a few minutes. Add the wine and stir until all the liquid has evaporated.

Pour in the hot chicken stock, add the salt and cover with the saucepan lid. Turn the heat to its lowest setting and cook for 14 minutes. Remove the lid. The rice should be slightly al dente but, if necessary, add a little extra stock and cook further.

Add the remaining lemon zest and any juice, the cream and Parmigiano Reggiano and stir well. Season with salt to taste. Set aside for a minute to allow the flavours to infuse, then add the lemon segments just before serving.

SERVES 4 AS AN ENTRÉE

SORREL SAUCE

Sorrel is an easy perennial herb to grow and is often used to accompany fish and white meats. In sauces its sourness helps to lift the flavour. Because it discolours quickly, however, it is best added at the last minute. This robust sauce will give a wonderful lift to lightly steamed, poached or fried fish, veal and chicken or to pan-fried haloumi.

1 clove garlic
1 teaspoon capers
½ teaspoon Dijon mustard
3 tablespoons crème fraîche
1 teaspoon lemon juice
salt and freshly ground black pepper
1 loosely packed cup sorrel leaves,
   stems removed

Combine all the ingredients in a food processor and pulse until smooth. Serve cold.

MAKES APPROXIMATELY 1 CUP

GREEN YOGHURT SAUCE

This is based on the Middle-Eastern borani: a spinach and yoghurt dip. It is particularly good with merguez lamb sausages, but it is also very good with simple barbecued lamb chops. Vary the greens, depending on what's available. If using spinach, blanch it first. This recipe makes quite a thick sauce, but it can be thinned down with extra yoghurt. It is best eaten on the day it is made.

pinch saffron
2 tablespoons olive oil
1 medium-sized onion, finely chopped
½ cup well-packed mixed greens (such
   as mint, rocket, parsley, watercress,
   spring onions, spinach)
½ cup thick Greek-style yoghurt, extra
   if desired
salt and freshly ground black pepper

Soak the saffron in a tablespoon of boiling water. In a sauté pan, heat the oil, add the onion and cook until softened but not coloured. Cool, then place in a food processor with the remaining ingredients (including the saffron liquid) and blend until smooth. If possible, set aside for 30 minutes to allow the flavours to develop. Serve in a bowl.

MAKES APPROXIMATELY 1½ CUPS

Spanish Snowpea Salad

This salad is based on a Spanish recipe using broad beans, but is equally as good using snowpeas or a mixture of broad beans and snowpeas. If possible choose white onions for their mild flavour or use shallots, spring onions or mild red onions. Guindillas are green peppers pickled in vinegar, water and salt.

500g snowpeas
3 tablespoons finely chopped
   white onion
2 cups diced tomato
4 tablespoons roughly chopped
   coriander leaves
1 teaspoon finely chopped
   oregano leaves
6 tablespoons (90ml) lime juice
4 tablespoons Spanish olive oil
1–2 fresh red chillies, seeded
   and finely sliced

For the topping
3 tablespoons chopped
   coriander leaves
½ cup onion rings
guindillas in brine, left whole
   (optional)

To prepare the snowpeas, snap off the stems and remove the string from each side of the pods. Blanch quickly in rapidly boiling salted water for about 90 seconds, until they turn bright green. Drain them and refresh under cold water. Place on paper towels and pat dry.

Toss together the snowpeas, onion, tomato, first measure of coriander, oregano, lime juice, oil and chilli. Set aside out of the refrigerator to marinate for an hour before serving.

To serve, sprinkle coriander, onion rings and guindillas (if using) on top. Serve cold.

Serves 6 as a salad

Pea And Spinach Soup

An easy-to-make soup that is light and fresh. It will taste a little more mellow if made ahead and allowed to rest overnight but the colour will not be quite as brilliant a green as it will if you make it at the last minute. Serve with toasted pita bread, cut into wedges.

30g butter
2 large onions, finely chopped
1 heaped teaspoon curry powder
    (any good commercial curry will do)
small bunch coriander leaves,
    roughly chopped
small bunch mint leaves, roughly
    chopped
1 litre vegetable stock or water
2 cups frozen baby peas
4 cups spinach leaves, stems discarded
    and finely sliced
½ cup coconut milk
salt and freshly ground black pepper
extra mint and coriander leaves
    for garnish

Melt the butter in a large saucepan. Over a low heat, gently fry the onions with the curry powder for about five minutes, until golden and soft. Add the coriander, mint and stock or water and simmer for about 10 minutes. Add the peas and spinach, bring to a boil and allow to simmer for three minutes.

Strain the mixture, returning the liquid to the rinsed-out pan. Place half the spinach and pea mixture in a food processor and process until it becomes a smooth purée. Combine this with the remaining spinach and pea mixture so that the consistency is chunky. Tip all this back into the liquid in the pan, combine well and stir in the coconut milk. The recipe can be prepared ahead to this point.

Reheat, stirring gently, and season with salt and pepper. Serve in heated bowls with the mint and coriander leaves piled on top of the soup.

Serves 6 as a lunch dish

SPINACH AND LEEK CRÊPES

This is a surprisingly rich dish that is suitable served for lunch with a crisp green salad. It can be made even more luxurious with cheese added to the mix — try some grated Gruyère or feta.

    Velouté is a classic French sauce. Equal parts of butter and flour are cooked together. A light stock is added to this 'roux' and cooked until the sauce is thick and velvety.

FOR THE CRÊPES
125g flour
2 eggs, lightly beaten
300ml milk
2 teaspoons olive oil
butter

FOR THE SPINACH AND LEEK FILLING
500g spinach, stems removed
1 tablespoon (15g) butter
2 leeks, halved lengthwise and thinly sliced
a grating of nutmeg
1 lemon, zest only

FOR THE VELOUTÉ
2 tablespoons (30g) butter
2 tablespoons flour
½ cup dry white wine
1½ cups chicken or vegetable stock plus a little extra

To make the crêpes, place the flour in a bowl. Whisk in the eggs and milk. Strain the batter to get rid of any lumps, then add the olive oil. The batter should be the consistency of cream. Refrigerate for at least two hours.

Heat a 20cm crêpe pan and melt a small knob of butter. Swirl it around to coat, then wipe clean with a paper towel. Pour in a small amount of batter and tip the pan to get an even coating. Cook until the crêpe begins to colour at the edges, then use a small palette knife to turn the crêpe over. Cook for another minute, then place on a plate.

Don't despair if your first crêpe isn't successful; often the first one is really only suitable for seasoning the pan. Wipe the pan clean with the butter-soaked paper towel and start again. The stack of crêpes can be refrigerated a day ahead if tightly wrapped in plastic wrap. They can also be frozen in layers with baking paper between each crêpe to stop them sticking together. The recipe makes 18 crêpes and this dish calls for 12, so six can be frozen and reserved for another use.

To make the filling, quickly wilt the spinach in a saucepan over a gentle heat, using only the water clinging to it from washing. Drain, allow to cool, then squeeze out any excess moisture. Melt the butter and gently sauté the leeks until they are soft but uncoloured. Mix with the spinach, adding the nutmeg and lemon zest.

For the velouté, make a roux by melting the butter in a medium-sized saucepan, then adding the flour and cooking gently until lightly coloured. Heat the wine and stock together and add slowly to the roux, whisking to prevent lumps. Simmer for 10 minutes or until lightly thickened. Mix half the velouté through the spinach mixture to moisten it. Reserve the rest to dress the crêpes.

Lay out 12 crêpes (two per person) on a bench. Divide the filling evenly between the crêpes (approximately three tablespoons in each crêpe), placing the mix in one quarter of the crêpe. Fold in half and then in half again. Place on a lightly buttered baking dish. (This recipe can be prepared ahead to this point.)

Preheat the oven to 180°C. Pour the rest of the velouté over the crêpes, then bake for 15 minutes or until heated through.

SERVES 6 AS A LUNCH DISH

SPINACH FRITTATA

The fresh dill and lemon zest, combined with careful seasoning, makes this spinach frittata a true spring lunch dish. Serve with a crisp green salad, crusty bread and an aromatic wine. Choose a 20cm ceramic, porcelain or Pyrex ovenproof dish, so the frittata cooks evenly.

8 bunches fresh spinach
  (approximately 350g bag),
  stems removed
25g butter
1 small onion, finely chopped
2 eggs
1 cup milk
¾ cup grated tasty cheddar
1 tablespoon chopped dill
1 lemon, zest only
salt and freshly ground black pepper
3 small tomatoes, seeded and
  coarsely chopped
1 tablespoon breadcrumbs,
  made from stale bread
1 tablespoon grated Parmigiano
  Reggiano

Wash the spinach, allowing any remaining water to cling to the leaves. Heat a medium-sized frying pan. Place the spinach in the pan without adding more water and cook over a medium heat, stirring occasionally, for 60 to 90 seconds or until the spinach has wilted. (This is best done in three or four batches to prevent overcooking.) Set aside in a colander to drain well.

Preheat the oven to 175°C. Lightly grease a 20cm baking dish. Melt the butter in the spinach pan and cook the onion for four to five minutes, until soft.

Whisk together the eggs, milk, cheese, dill and lemon zest. Season well with salt and pepper. Squeeze any excess moisture from the spinach and chop coarsely. Add to the egg mixture with the onion and tomatoes. Pour into the prepared dish, then sprinkle the breadcrumbs and cheese over the top.

Cook for 25 minutes until golden and set. Allow to stand for 10 minutes before serving.

SERVES 4 FOR LUNCH OR 6 AS A STARTER

Roasted Baby New Potatoes with Garlic and Thyme

The first of the new season's potatoes arrive at the end of the spring season. Baby potatoes are always delicious steamed but we love to roast them slowly with garlic and thyme, so they are tender and moreish. After we photographed this dish, the potatoes all disappeared in a few minutes!

1.5kg baby new potatoes (Jersey Bennes, Ruas or Red Rascals)
1 bulb garlic
15 small sprigs fresh lemon thyme
3 tablespoons olive oil
1 tablespoon sea salt
freshly ground black pepper

Preheat the oven to 220°C.

Slice the larger potatoes into halves. Separate the garlic into cloves but do not remove the skins. Very roughly chop the thyme sprigs.

Toss the potatoes into a roasting pan with the garlic and thyme. Sprinkle the olive oil and salt over the potatoes with several grinds of pepper, tossing well so the potatoes are thoroughly coated.

Bake in the oven for 50 to 60 minutes, until the potatoes are golden and their interiors soft and fluffy. Serve at once.

SERVES 6 TO ACCOMPANY A MAIN COURSE OR IN A SHARED MEAL

New Potato, Asparagus and Lemon Salad

This fabulous combination makes a lovely spring luncheon dish or could be used as an entrée or as part of a buffet. It's equally good made ahead, refrigerated and brought back to room temperature for serving.

500g baby new potatoes, scrubbed
salt and freshly ground black pepper
300g asparagus spears, peeled and cut
 into 6cm lengths
1 lemon, zest and juice, for dressing
6 tablespoons (60ml) olive oil
2 small chillies, seeded and very
 finely sliced
1 teaspoon Dijon mustard
small pinch sugar
salt and freshly ground black pepper
4 lemons, peeled with a knife and
 cut into segments
small bunch chives, cut into
 3cm lengths

Simmer the potatoes in a saucepan with enough salted water to cover them, cooking until tender. Drain.

Meanwhile, simmer the asparagus in another pan of salted water for three to four minutes. Drain and refresh under cold running water to retain the bright green colour.

Make a dressing by placing the lemon zest and juice, olive oil, chillies, mustard, sugar, salt and pepper in a bowl, then whisking together.

Place the warm potatoes, asparagus and lemon segments in a serving bowl. Toss very gently with the dressing to coat all ingredients, taking care not to break up the lemon or damage the asparagus. Scatter the chives over the top and serve.

Serves 4–6 as an entrée

SAFFRON ROASTED POTATOES

These gorgeous golden potatoes are best made with a good baking potato such as Agria. They are a great accompaniment to fish or chicken but also make a delicious tapas dish, either as they are or with sliced chorizo added to the baking dish in the last 15 minutes of roasting.

700g potatoes (Agria)
2 tablespoons olive oil
pinch saffron
sea salt

Preheat the oven to 220°C.

Peel the potatoes and halve or quarter them, depending on size. Heat the oil in a large saucepan, add the potatoes and saffron, then sauté until lightly golden. Season with salt, add half a cup of water, cover and cook gently for 10 minutes or until the water has evaporated.

Place the potatoes in a baking dish and roast for 45 minutes or until golden. Serve immediately.

SERVES 4–6 AS A SIDE DISH

SUMMER

IN SEASON: Beans, Corn, Cucumbers, Garlic, Peppers,
Radishes, Red Onions, Tomatoes, Zucchini and salads galore . . .

MINTY GREEN BEANS AND PEAS WITH FETA

This delicious vegetable mélange can complement meat or poultry or be served on its own as a starter.

1kg tender young green beans
2 cups frozen green peas
8 small zucchini, thinly sliced
1 cup chicken stock
2 tablespoons butter
salt and freshly ground black pepper
150g feta, crumbled
½ cup chopped mint leaves

Trim and slice the beans. Place all the vegetables in a saucepan with the chicken stock, and bring to a simmer. Allow to simmer for three to four minutes, until tender but still bright green. Drain over a bowl, catching the liquid.

Return the liquid to the pan with the butter and boil vigorously so that it reduces to about half a cup. Place the vegetables in a serving bowl, tip the reduced stock over them and season well. Garnish with the crumbled feta and fresh mint, and serve immediately

SERVES 8 AS A SIDE DISH OR IN A SHARED MEAL

GREEN BEANS WITH CITRUS BUTTER AND ALMONDS

This is an elegant yet simply prepared side dish. Substitute lemon juice for the orange juice if you prefer.

600g green beans, trimmed
1 orange, zest and juice
20g butter, softened
¼ cup toasted almonds
sea salt and freshly ground
   black pepper

Cook the beans in boiling water until tender. Drain and combine with the orange zest, juice and butter. Place in a serving dish, sprinkle the toasted almonds over the top and season with salt and pepper. Serve hot.

SERVES 6 AS A SIDE DISH

Bean Salad with Peppers and Red Onions

Peppers, beans and tomatoes: the perfect summer combination. The nuggets of white bean make this quite a substantial salad, and it is a good accompaniment for grilled meats and chicken.

2 red peppers
3 medium-sized red onions, cut into
  wedges
8 cloves garlic
300g round green beans
1 small punnet cherry tomatoes
560g jar preserved Italian white beans,
  well drained
2 handfuls rocket leaves
½ cup basil leaves
½ cup Italian parsley leaves

For the vinaigrette
4 very ripe tomatoes, peeled and seeded
6 tablespoons (90ml) extra virgin
  olive oil
1 small onion, finely chopped
1 teaspoon smoked paprika
2 tablespoons sherry vinegar
salt and freshly ground black pepper
pinch sugar

Preheat the oven to 190°C. Cut the peppers in half, remove the seeds and stalks and put in a roasting pan with the wedges of onion and the whole garlic cloves. Bake for 25 minutes, then remove the garlic, peel and set aside.

Continue roasting the peppers and onion for a further 15 minutes, until they are soft and well cooked. Cool, then remove and discard the skin from the peppers. Chop the peppers roughly. Set them and the onion aside.

Trim the beans and cut them in half unless they are quite small. Blanch in salted boiling water for two minutes, then remove, refresh and put aside. Cut the cherry tomatoes in half.

To assemble the salad, toss the white beans, green beans, peppers, onions and garlic cloves in a bowl. Add the cherry tomatoes, rocket, basil and parsley leaves.

To make the tomato vinaigrette, purée the tomatoes. Place one tablespoon of the oil in a small pan, add the onion and paprika, and cook very gently until the onion is well softened.

Place the fresh tomato purée, onion mixture and sherry vinegar in a small bowl and whisk together well. Season with salt, pepper and a pinch of sugar, then add the remaining olive oil, a little at a time. Toss the salad lightly with the vinaigrette.

Serves 6 as a starter salad or side dish

FRESH CORN ON THE COB WITH GARLIC BUTTER AND PARMESAN

A simple way to cook corn, resulting in very juicy corn with a nutty flavour. The butter will freeze well.

100g butter, softened
1–2 cloves garlic, crushed
2 tablespoons finely chopped coriander
　or Italian parsley
6 corn cobs, husks and silks removed
2 tablespoons extra virgin olive oil
salt and freshly ground black pepper
grated Parmigiano Reggiano

Mix together the softened butter, garlic and herbs. Place in a ramekin or make a butter roll by placing in a piece of baking paper or plastic wrap and rolling into a cigar shape. Chill to firm up the butter, then cut into small rounds.

Preheat a barbecue grill or ridged griddle. Rub the corn cobs with the oil and sprinkle with salt and pepper. Place on the hot grill and cook for 15 minutes, turning regularly.

Serve the corn with the butter and plenty of grated Parmigiano Reggiano — and pass the pepper grinder.

SERVES 6 AS A SIDE DISH

SUMMER PASTA SALAD

Whip up this salad for unexpected guests or a crowd. It is a store-cupboard-meets-garden creation: you can use whatever vegetables are fresh from the market. The punchy flavour of the herb dressing makes it a true taste of summer. When making a pasta salad, avoid using too much pasta or it becomes heavy and starchy. The emphasis should be on the vegetables.

2 cups (250g) pasta shapes (farfalle or similar)

½ cup each chopped basil, parsley and coriander

2 lemons, zest and juice

2 teaspoons Dijon mustard

½ cup extra virgin olive oil

plenty of salt and freshly ground black pepper

2 tablespoons olive oil, for the pasta

2 firm avocados, peeled and cut into chunks

1 cup cherry tomatoes, halved

300g tender young green beans, trimmed and blanched

corn kernels cut from 2 cooked corn cobs

1 cup young trimmed watercress leaves

Cook the pasta in plenty of boiling salted water until tender or al dente.

Meanwhile, make the dressing by placing the herbs (not the watercress), lemon zest and juice in a food processor with the mustard. Combine well, then add the extra virgin olive oil through the feed tube with the motor running until it is all combined. Season well with salt and pepper to taste.

When the pasta is cooked, immediately drain it and toss in a little olive oil to stop the pieces sticking together.

To serve, gently toss the pasta with the dressing, add the remaining ingredients and toss gently until everything is well mixed but not mushy. Serve with crusty bread. This salad can be served warm, or cooled to room temperature.

SERVES 8 FOR LUNCH, MORE IN A SHARED MEAL

Hot Cucumber with Fresh Dill

Cucumber cooked as a vegetable is not common in New Zealand but is delicious served with lamb cutlets and buttery new potatoes. Steaming cucumber turns this vegetable a vibrant green. You could substitute dill seeds for leaves in this recipe, but use only a good pinch.

1–2 telegraph cucumbers, depending
  on size
50g butter
1 lemon, juice
1–2 tablespoons chopped fresh dill

Peel the cucumber, cut in half lengthwise and remove the seeds using a teaspoon. Cut into chunks or thick slices.

Steam the cucumber chunks or slices until tender, about three minutes.

In a frying pan, melt the butter and toss with the cucumber over heat until the cucumber is well coated with golden butter. Add the lemon juice and dill and serve immediately.

SERVES 6 AS A SIDE DISH

Summer Salad of Cucumber, Medjool Dates, Roasted Peppers and Walnuts

This juicy and succulent salad makes a delicious accompaniment to simply grilled fish fillets.

2 peppers (any colour except green)
olive oil
½ cucumber
½ cup Medjool dates, halved and
  stones removed
½ cup shelled walnut halves
2 tablespoons lemon juice
3 tablespoons extra virgin olive oil,
  for dressing
sea salt and freshly ground black
  pepper
2 tablespoons shredded mint

Preheat the oven to 190°C. Place the peppers in a roasting pan, brush with olive oil and bake for about 25 minutes, until they are soft and well cooked. Cool, then remove and discard the skins, cores and seeds. Rip the peppers into strips and set aside.

Taste the skin of the cucumber and if it is bitter, peel and discard it. Cut into quarters lengthwise, remove the seeds, then slice on the diagonal. Put in a bowl with the peppers, dates and walnuts.

Make a dressing with the lemon juice, olive oil and salt and pepper. Dress the salad, add the mint and serve immediately.

Serves 4 as a side dish

Warm Salad of Carrots and Slow-Cooked Red Peppers

The warm colours and lovely fresh flavours make this a delicious sweet vegetable dish. This dish can be served either hot or at room temperature.

500g carrots, peeled and sliced into
   small batons
6 tablespoons (90ml) extra virgin
   olive oil
1 large red onion, finely sliced
3 red peppers, seeded and veins
   removed, sliced into neat strips
2 tablespoons red wine vinegar
2 teaspoons runny floral honey
salt and freshly ground black pepper
1 tablespoon finely chopped
   Italian parsley

Place the carrots in a saucepan with water to cover and bring to a boil. Simmer until the carrots are tender. Drain and keep aside.

Put two tablespoons of the olive oil in a frying pan and heat until hot. Add the onion, lower the heat and cook gently until the onion starts to soften. Add the strips of pepper and continue to cook over gentle heat for at least 20 minutes, until the peppers are soft and sweet. Remove from the heat.

Make a vinaigrette by mixing the red wine vinegar with the remaining olive oil, the honey and salt and pepper to taste.

Combine all the vegetables in a serving dish, dress with the vinaigrette and sprinkle the chopped parsley over the top.

SERVES 6 AS A SIDE DISH

Roasted Pepper and Ricotta Terrine with Salad

This ricotta loaf can be prepared a day or two ahead. The cheesy flavour is balanced by the roasted peppers. It may sound rich but it is a light and airy way to start a meal, and as a main it goes beautifully with salad and crusty bread. Perfect with Sauvignon Blanc.

2 red peppers
2 yellow peppers
750g ricotta
250g sour cream or crème fraîche
4 eggs, beaten
1 cup grated Parmigiano Reggiano
pinch nutmeg
2 tablespoons chopped thyme
salt and freshly ground black pepper

For the salad
½ cup finely chopped parsley
½ cup finely chopped basil
1 lemon, juice and grated zest
¼ cup extra virgin olive oil
salt and freshly ground black pepper
salad leaves including cos,
  buttercrunch and rocket

Preheat the oven to 200°C. Roast the peppers until the skins darken and begin to blister. When the peppers are cool, remove the skins, seeds and veins and cut the flesh into strips.

To make the terrine, reduce the oven heat to 180°C. Line a deep 25cm loaf tin with baking paper. Beat the ricotta until smooth, add the sour cream and eggs, and beat to combine well. Stir in the grated Parmigiano Reggiano, then season with the nutmeg, thyme, salt and pepper.

Spoon one-third of the cheese mixture into the lined tin. Top this with the red pepper strips. Cover with another third of the mixture. Place the yellow pepper strips on this and cover with the remaining mixture.

Cover the tin with a layer of foil. Bake for 55 minutes, testing to make sure the mixture is firm: touch the top lightly with your fingers; it will spring back when cooked. Allow to cool, then refrigerate until needed.

Before serving, return the terrine to room temperature, drain any excess liquid off and turn out on a serving platter. Make a dressing by combining the finely chopped herbs with the lemon juice and zest, olive oil, and salt and pepper to taste.

Cut the terrine into slices, spoon a little of the herby dressing over these, and serve with crusty bread and a small salad of freshly picked leaves.

Serves 8 as a lunch dish

Stuffed Peppers

Choose large fleshy peppers that are ripe but still firm for this dish. These are baked in the oven and make a superb summer first course. For a main course, they can star with green salad or complement meat. Vegetable dishes are always great with chilled Sauvignon Blanc.

6 large firm ripe peppers
3 tablespoons extra virgin olive oil
8 shallots, peeled and finely chopped
2 zucchini, chopped finely
3 cups cooked basmati rice
   (approximately 1½ cups raw)
2 tablespoons chopped thyme
2 tablespoons chopped parsley
1 lemon, zest and juice
salt and freshly ground black pepper
2 medium-sized tomatoes, peeled
200g feta, crumbled
2 tablespoons grated pecorino cheese

Slice the tops of the peppers across, about 1cm deep. With a very sharp knife, cut out the inside veins and seeds, and discard. Take care not to pierce the sides of the peppers.

Preheat the oven to 180°C.

To make the stuffing, heat the olive oil in a large frying pan. Add the shallots and cook gently until they soften. Add the chopped zucchini and continue to cook so that the moisture is evaporated. Remove this mixture from the heat and add to the rice with the thyme, parsley, lemon zest and juice, salt and pepper.

Roughly chop the tomatoes and add to the mixture with the feta. The stuffing should be moist but not soggy. Taste and adjust the seasoning if necessary.

Stuff this mixture into the peppers, and top with the grated pecorino. Bake for about 25 minutes, until the stuffing is nicely browned and the peppers are well cooked through.

Serves 6 as a main dish with a salad

TUSCAN PEACH AND PROSCIUTTO SALAD

This entrée is popular in Tuscany. Some versions use walnuts and walnut oil. We prefer to use toasted almonds, which are a better complement to the peaches; nectarines will also work well here. It is not necessary to remove the skin of the tomatoes and peaches, though it does make for a more elegant starter. What is essential is that you use really good-quality, perfectly ripe peaches and tomatoes.

500g tomatoes, peeled, halved or
    quartered, depending on size
500g peaches, peeled and stoned
1 tablespoon lemon juice
2 tablespoons extra virgin olive oil
sea salt and freshly ground
    black pepper
40g toasted almonds
12 very thin slices prosciutto

Cut the tomatoes and peaches into wedges of the same size. Toss with the lemon juice and olive oil, and season well with salt and pepper. Divide between four plates, scatter the almonds over the top and arrange three slices of prosciutto on each plate. Serve immediately.

SERVES 4 AS A STARTER

ORZO SALAD WITH YELLOW PEPPER AND LEMON

A light, refreshing salad with the surprise addition of ricotta. Great with barbecued snapper or similar fish (with skin on).

½ cup extra virgin olive oil
2 lemons, zest and juice
salt and freshly ground black pepper
2 cups orzo
2 small yellow peppers, seeded and
  finely diced
1 Lebanese (or ½ small telegraph)
  cucumber, seeded and finely diced
100g ricotta, crumbled
3–4 tablespoons mint leaves, torn

To make the dressing, combine the oil, lemon zest and juice in a large bowl. Season with salt and pepper.

Cook the orzo in a large saucepan of boiling water until al dente, about 10 to 12 minutes. Drain in a fine colander and run under cold water. Drain well a second time then add to the dressing, mix well and allow to cool.

Mix in the peppers, cucumber, ricotta and mint until well combined. Place in a large serving bowl and serve immediately.

SERVES 6 AS A MAIN COURSE

PANZANELLA

Prepare this Tuscan salad a couple of hours ahead to allow the flavours to blend together. If you wish, add a red chilli (seeded and finely chopped) and six to eight anchovy fillets. Perfect for an alfresco meal — a picnic with cold sliced meats, or with meat hot off the barbecue.

2 teaspoons salted capers
2 red peppers
2 yellow peppers
1 clove garlic, crushed
2–3 tablespoons red wine vinegar
6 tablespoons (90ml) extra virgin
   olive oil
salt and freshly ground black pepper
200g (approximately ½ loaf) good-
   quality ciabatta, one day old
6 tomatoes
1 red onion, thinly sliced
½ cup pitted black olives
   (we used Ligurian)
1 cup basil leaves, approximately

Preheat the oven to 200°C. Soak the capers for 30 minutes, then rinse them well. Remove the green stems and cores from the peppers and wash well to remove the white seeds inside, then dry.

Place the peppers in a shallow roasting dish lined with baking paper and roast until the skin is well blistered, turning once. Alternatively, roast on a barbecue or under a hot grill. Allow to cool before peeling away and discarding the skin. Cut the flesh into slices.

In a small bowl, combine the garlic and vinegar. Whisk in the olive oil, then season with salt and black pepper to taste.

Cut the ciabatta into cubes and toast under a grill. Cut the tomatoes in half horizontally, then quarter each half. In a large salad bowl, combine the tomatoes, onion, roasted peppers and toasted bread.

Pour in the red wine vinaigrette, capers and olives. Taste for seasoning and adjust if necessary. Cover and refrigerate for at least two hours. Serve sprinkled with the basil leaves.

SERVES 6 AS A STARTER OR SIDE DISH

PISSALADIÈRE

A classic from Nice, in Provence, made in this recipe with a base of simple pizza dough. Serve it for lunch with a green salad. When making the dough, have everything warm and work in a draught-free place. Use the same dough for margherita pizza — topped with tomato sauce, buffalo mozzarella and basil, cooked then finished with rocket and Parmigiano Reggiano.

FOR THE DOUGH

1 teaspoon sugar
3 teaspoons dried yeast (we used Edmonds Active Yeast)
4 tablespoons warm water
3 cups high-grade flour
1 teaspoon salt
¾ cup warm water

FOR THE TOPPING

4 large onions, sliced
2 tablespoons olive oil
16 anchovies, halved lengthwise
24 black olives, approximately (we used Kalamata)
extra olive oil for drizzling

To make the dough, place the sugar and yeast in a small bowl, then add the four tablespoons of warm water. Leave until it foams, about five minutes.

Sift the flour with the salt into the bowl of an electric mixer. Pour in the yeast mixture and the second measure of warm water.

Using the dough-hook of the mixer, electrically knead the dough until it is smooth and shiny, about 10 minutes. If the dough appears dry, add a little more water. If kneading by hand, mix to a soft dough then turn out on to a floured benchtop and knead. Use extra flour only if necessary: the wetter the better.

Lightly oil a large bowl and place the dough in it, turning once. Cover with a tea towel and let rise in a warm place until double in volume, about one hour.

While the dough is proving, begin preparing the topping. Slowly cook the onions in the olive oil until very soft (30 to 45 minutes).

Preheat the oven to 200°C. Knock back the dough and place on a lightly oiled shallow baking tray (30cm x 20cm).

Press the dough with your hands to fit the tray, leaving the outside rim slightly thicker. Leaving a 1cm rim, lay the onion slices on the dough. Arrange anchovy strips in rows to form large diamonds. Place an olive in the centre of each diamond and drizzle a little oil on top.

Bake for 20 minutes, until the dough is brown and crisp. Serve either hot or warm.

SERVES 6 AS A LUNCH DISH

Fennel, Feta, Olive and Lemon Tart

With a block of puff pastry in the freezer, any cook can whip up a substantial lunch dish (accompanied by a salad) or a great starter for friends who pop in unexpectedly. The tart can be topped with all sorts of interesting things from the garden or the store cupboard, and is best kept really simple.

500g puff pastry
1 egg, beaten
3 bulbs fennel, trimmed and
   sliced paper thin
2 teaspoons fennel seeds
150g crumbly feta cheese
½ cup olives, pitted
1 preserved lemon, zest only, diced
sea salt and freshly ground black
   pepper
handful Italian parsley leaves,
   stems removed

Roll out the pastry to fit a 30cm x 40cm oven tray. Allow the pastry to rest in the refrigerator for at least 30 minutes. Preheat the oven to 200°C.

Beat the egg and brush it over the surface of the pastry. Layer the fennel on the pastry and scatter the seeds over the top. Crumble the cheese over the fennel next, and then dot the top with olives and preserved lemon dice. Season with salt and pepper.

Place the tart in the hot oven and turn the heat up to 210°C so the pastry really starts to cook. When the pastry is puffed and golden brown on the edges and underside (in about 20 minutes, depending on your oven) remove the tart from the oven. Scatter the parsley leaves over the whole and cut into generous wedges (or small squares, for starters) to serve.

SERVES 6 AS A MAIN COURSE OR MAKES UP TO 24 SMALL STARTERS

SUMMER ROASTED VEGETABLE TART

This will make a lovely brunch or lunch dish. The vegetables can be replaced with others such as red peppers, aubergines, beans or whatever is available that is fresh and lovely.

400g puff pastry
2 medium-sized bulbs fennel, trimmed
1 red onion
4 small potatoes
2 zucchini
2 tablespoons extra virgin olive oil
salt and freshly ground black pepper
4 eggs
6 tablespoons crème fraîche
3 medium-sized tomatoes, sliced
½ cup finely chopped parsley
  and basil

Roll the puff pastry out thinly and line a 24cm loose-bottomed flan tin, bringing the pastry up to the top and slightly over the edge. Prick the base and refrigerate to rest for at least 30 minutes.

Preheat the oven to 200°C. Cut the vegetables (except the tomatoes) into small pieces about 3cm square. Place them in an oven tray with the olive oil, salt and pepper and bake for about 15 minutes, until soft and cooked through. Remove from the oven, leaving the oven on, and cool the vegetables.

Before cooking the tart, place an oven tray in the oven and turn the heat up to 220°C. (When you place the tart tin on the heated tray, the pastry at the bottom will cook through.)

Fill the tart shell with the cooled vegetables. Beat the eggs with the crème fraîche, add salt and pepper and pour over the vegetables. Arrange slices of fresh tomato on top of this and scatter the chopped herbs over everything. Bake for 45 minutes or until puffed and golden. Serve warm.

SERVES 8 AS A STARTER OR LUNCH DISH

Radishes with Bread and Butter

Our favourite way of eating radishes is to arrange them in a bowl or on a plate (leaving just enough green leafage to hold them by), with a small bowl of coarse sea salt and a basket of bread. Butter the radish, rather than the bread, then dip it into the salt. Add a sprinkling of fennel seeds to the salt if you wish.

If the radishes you buy are not as crisp as you would like, put them in a bowl of iced water and leave for about two hours.

Radishes with Oranges

These make a lovely light refreshing salad to serve when radishes are fresh and crisp.

6 radishes, sliced thinly
3 oranges, peeled and sliced
salt
1 lemon, juice only

Cut the radishes and oranges into evenly sized pieces (smallish) and arrange on a large flat plate. Season with a little salt, drizzle the lemon juice over the top and serve.

SERVES 6 IN A SHARED MEAL

Fresh Tomato Salad with Lemon and Basil

During the summer, sweet, ripe outdoor-grown tomatoes can be found in the farmers' markets and at vegetable stands in the country. We love to use the heirloom varieties, with their lovely colours and unusual shapes. Simply dress them like this with lemon zest, basil and olive oil. There's no need to use any vinegar or lemon juice as tomatoes have plenty of natural acidity. Perfect with a fruity Riesling and to accompany grilled meat or fish in a main course.

2kg mixed ripe tomatoes, chosen from: large beefsteak tomatoes; yellow, orange or red cherry tomatoes; heirloom varieties; Roma tomatoes
1 red onion, sliced paper thin
1 lemon, zest only
salt and freshly ground black pepper
pinch sugar
4 tablespoons light, fruity extra virgin olive oil
6–8 large basil leaves, finely sliced

Wash and dry the tomatoes, then cut them into pieces or slices. Arrange the tomatoes on a large flat plate; don't pile them on top of each other, as they can become 'clammy'.

Sprinkle the onion slices and lemon zest over the tomatoes and season with plenty of salt and pepper and a little sugar. Finally, drizzle the olive oil and scatter basil leaves over the top.

SERVES 8 AS A STARTER OR SIDE DISH

Raw Tomato and Basil Sauce on Spaghetti

In the time that it takes to bring a saucepan of water to the boil to cook the pasta, this sauce is made. It's a fuss-free dish that makes for easy family meals. Use the best tomatoes you can find and a really good fruity olive oil. A good addition to the dish would be salami or pancetta, cut into matchsticks and fried until crisp.

400g dried spaghetti
4 tablespoons extra virgin olive oil
1 small clove garlic, peeled
sea salt
600g tomatoes
1 large handful basil leaves, stems
   removed
25g Parmigiano Reggiano, grated
extra grated Parmigiano Reggiano
   for serving

Bring a saucepan of water to the boil, add plenty of salt, bring back to the boil and add the spaghetti. Cook according to the instructions on the packet, until al dente. Drain well, reserving a little of the cooking water.

While the pasta is cooking, pour the olive oil into a large bowl. Using the side of your knife, mash the garlic to a paste with a little sea salt and add to the oil. Roughly chop the tomatoes and add to the bowl with the basil leaves.

When the pasta is cooked and drained, add to the bowl and toss together gently. Add a little of the reserved cooking water to the bowl if the sauce seems a little dry (it is tempting to add more oil but it makes the finished dish too oily), then toss through the Parmigiano Reggiano. Taste and adjust the seasonings if necessary.

Serve immediately with extra Parmigiano Reggiano.

SERVES 4 AS A MAIN DISH

Cherry Tomato Salad with Sun-Dried Tomato Dressing

This delicious yet simple salad is given extra depth through the use of sun-dried tomatoes. It makes a good accompaniment to grilled meats and fish.

For the dressing
2 sun-dried tomatoes, chopped
1 clove garlic, peeled
1 tablespoon red wine vinegar
3 tablespoons extra virgin olive oil
2 tablespoons cream
sea salt

For the salad
2 punnets cherry tomatoes, halved
small handful basil leaves

Pulse the sun-dried tomatoes and garlic in a food processor. Add the remaining dressing ingredients and process to a smooth consistency. Season to taste.

Toss the cherry tomatoes, basil and dressing together. Serve immediately.

Serves 6 as a side dish

Tomato Bruschetta with Salmoriglio

This very simple bruschetta is perfect for relaxed summer entertaining, and the sauce is a Sicilian classic. Grill the bruschetta as required, and serve with a platter of vegetables, such as raw radishes, fennel bulbs and celery, and a mix of marinated vegetables, possibly some cured meats, olives and a good cheese or two.

For the salmoriglio

1 clove garlic, peeled
¼ cup tightly packed marjoram,
  oregano or basil leaves
pinch sea salt
½ lemon, juice only
¼ cup extra virgin olive oil

For the bruschetta

1 loaf day-old sourdough or ciabatta,
  sliced
1 clove garlic, cut in half
tomatoes (½ per slice of bread),
  cut in half
extra virgin olive oil (use your best
  and don't stint on it)
sea salt and freshly ground black pepper

To make the salmoriglio, pound the garlic with the marjoram and a little salt in a mortar (or crush the salt and garlic with the flat of a knife and chop the herbs) until you have a smooth paste. Add the lemon juice and olive oil.

To prepare the bruschetta, grill the bread then rub each piece all over with garlic. Squeeze the cut side of the tomatoes over the bread (you can discard the skin if you like). Pour some olive oil over the top and drizzle with a little of the salmoriglio. Serve immediately.

Serves 6 as a starter

OVEN-BAKED SEMI-DRIED TOMATOES

This recipe is ideal for using a surplus of tomatoes. Pack them into a jar, cover them with a light fruity olive oil, and use them for soups, stews and just to eat as a treat.

¼ cup extra virgin olive oil
2kg ripe Roma tomatoes
2 tablespoons thyme leaves
2 teaspoons salt
2 teaspoons caster sugar
additional extra virgin olive oil
    for preserving

Preheat the oven to 150°C. Drizzle a little of the olive oil over a large baking tray.

Cut the tomatoes into halves lengthwise. Using a knife, remove and discard most of the pulp and the seeds, leaving the tomatoes with little hollows.

Drizzle a little more olive oil over each half, and sprinkle with thyme leaves, salt and caster sugar.

Put in the oven for about 45 minutes. Remove and allow to cool.

The tomatoes are now ready to eat, to use in salads or stews — or to pack into a sterilised jar and cover with light fruity olive oil. You can keep them refrigerated for up to two weeks.

MAKES 1 LITRE

ROASTED RED PEPPER AND TOMATO SAUCE

This simple sauce is excellent with pork sausages or to accompany pan-fried haloumi and crusty bread.

2 red peppers
2 tomatoes
1 clove garlic
pinch sweet smoked paprika
sea salt

Preheat the oven to 180°C.

Roast the peppers and tomatoes until the tomatoes are squishy (about 30 minutes, depending on size) and the peppers are blackened (35 to 40 minutes). Remove and cool. When cool enough to handle, discard the skins and seeds from both, then pulse in a food processor with the remaining ingredients until smooth.

MAKES ABOUT 1 CUP

OLD-FASHIONED TOMATO SAUCE

Many of us grew up with the smell of vinegar wafting through the house as our mothers made tomato sauce. And the taste of home-bottled sauce (or ketchup) is so good. It's the perfect store cupboard essential, making the most of summer's bounty.

5kg ripe tomatoes, roughly chopped
1.5kg onions, roughly chopped
2 tablespoons salt
500g soft brown sugar
500g white sugar
6cm piece ginger, peeled and crushed
4 cloves garlic, peeled
2 litres spiced vinegar

Place all the ingredients except the vinegar in a large preserving pan. Bring to a boil and simmer steadily for two hours. Cool and put through a mouli sieve.

Wash out the preserving pan and return the purée to it, adding the vinegar. Bring back to a boil and simmer steadily for another 30 minutes, until it reaches a thick consistency.

Ladle into sterilised jars or bottles and cover tightly with clean lid.

The quantity made depends on the juice content of the tomatoes and the evaporation during the boiling process. The sauce will keep for up to one year.

MAKES 2–3 LITRES

Tomato, Cannellini Beans and Rosemary Risotto

This dish is perfect for cooler summer days. Serve a salad of bitter greens (such as rocket, radicchio, witloof and watercress) afterwards.

40g butter
2 tablespoons olive oil
2 onions, finely chopped
4 large tomatoes (approximately 500g)
2 cloves garlic, finely chopped
1 teaspoon finely chopped rosemary
1 cup vialone nano, carnaroli or
    Arborio rice (Ferron brand)
½ cup dry white wine
2 cups chicken or vegetable stock,
    hot (more if needed)
400g tin cannellini beans, drained
    and rinsed
25g Parmigiano Reggiano, finely grated
sea salt and freshly ground black pepper
extra Parmigiano Reggiano for serving

Heat half the butter and olive oil in a wide saucepan, add the onions and fry gently until soft but not coloured (about 10 minutes). While the onions are cooking, blanch the tomatoes in boiling water for 15 seconds then plunge into cold water to arrest cooking. Remove the skins, halve the tomatoes and scoop out the juice and seeds, straining the juice through a sieve into a bowl. Discard the seeds but keep the tomato juice. Chop the remaining tomato flesh finely.

Add the garlic and rosemary to the onion and cook for a few minutes. Add the tomatoes and cook until quite thick (about five minutes). Add the rice, stir and coat in the tomato sauce. Add the wine and stir until all the liquid has evaporated.

Add the tomato juice to the hot stock then add a ladleful of this mixture to the risotto. Stir constantly until all the liquid is absorbed before adding the next ladleful. The risotto should be kept at a rapid simmer. Repeat, a ladle at a time, until the rice is al dente (about 20 minutes, but start checking after 15).

Add the cannellini beans and cook until heated through. Off the heat, add the remaining butter and the Parmigiano Reggiano. Set aside for a minute to allow the flavours to infuse, then serve immediately with a sprinkling of extra grated Parmigiano Reggiano.

Serves 4 as a main course

SUMMER MEANS . . . TOMATOES

No vegetable delivers the brilliant combination of both savoury and sweet sensations offered by a freshly plucked, ripe and juicy tomato. And the tomato is truly versatile.

Salads, soups, sauces and stews made with tomatoes can become the centrepiece of meals and snacks. As crops ripen during the height of the summer harvest, look for the wonderful array of heritage tomatoes in the farmers' markets, or, better still, harvest your own. This is the time to put away what is essentially the essence of summer, so you can draw on it all year round.

ALL ABOUT TOMATOES

CHOOSING AND STORING

Look for firm but ripe tomatoes that feel quite heavy in the hand: these will have a denser interior with a lower proportion of water.

Tomatoes are picked by the grower when half ripe and will continue to ripen to ideal condition over the next three or four days. A little green colouring on the top of the tomato will mean you can ripen it over two or three days.

Avoid tomatoes with 'ghost' spotting (Botrytis spores in early growth cause this), russeting and split skins (both caused by poor temperature control while growing).

Ideal storage conditions are between 11°C and 14°C, as for stonefruit. The average temperature in the bottom of a refrigerator is 4°C. Keep tomatoes out of the fridge or their acid will convert to sugar as soon as they are removed, resulting in soft tomatoes.

ENHANCING THE FLAVOUR

With so much natural acidity, tomatoes cry out for a pinch of sugar to improve their flavour. We cannot think of a single tomato salad or cooked dish that is not enhanced by adding sugar. Salt is also needed to develop the flavour, especially when a tomato comes up short of being really ripe.

HOW TO PEEL A TOMATO

Peeling a tomato for a salad is unnecessary, unless the skins are tough and thick.

Heat a large pot of water to boiling point. Fill a bowl with ice-cold water. Cut a small cross at the bottom of each tomato, then plunge the tomatoes into the boiling water for 10 seconds. Remove with kitchen tongs and immediately plunge the tomatoes into the ice-cold water to stop any cooking or softening. The skins should now peel easily.

Ripe tomatoes can also be held over a gas flame so that the skin blisters and loosens. Cool, then peel.

TOMATO PRODUCTS AND THEIR USES

PASSATA DI POMODORO: Usually sold in cans or jars and made from tomatoes that have been puréed (often cooked lightly) so that skins, seeds and excess water are removed. Use in sauces, stews, soups and gravies. Use within a day or two of opening.

TOMATO PASTE: Highly concentrated tomato purée. Sold in jars and cans, but best of all in tubes that prevent air entering and can be stored in the refrigerator for weeks. Use to boost the flavour of any dish — a couple of tablespoons are all that's needed.

TOMATO SAUCE: Sometimes called 'ketchup'. Slightly spicy preserved sauces are available commercially and are used worldwide as a flavour enhancer for meats, hamburgers, fish and chips and many other foods.

SUGO DI POMODORO: Italian term for a light tomato sauce that can be tossed over pasta or used in the making of a more complex sauce.

DRIED TOMATOES: Sun-dried in natural sunlight, or dehydrated wholly or semi-dried in a hot or warm oven, these tomatoes develop intense flavour. If fully dried the tomatoes can be stored in airtight conditions. Dried and semi-dried tomatoes can be covered with olive oil for storage.

CANNED TOMATOES: The best we have found are from Italy, as there the tomatoes are grown on low bushes and are left to ripen and dry in the fields, developing what tomato growers call DWM (dry weight matter). This means they are dense with little moisture and intensely developed flavour.

Canned tomatoes, whether the local flavoured brands or the imported tomatoes, are a pantry staple for cooking.

FRESH TOMATO TIPS

◆ Slice tomatoes and top with extra virgin olive oil, salt, freshly ground black pepper and very thin slices of shallot.

◆ Place thickly sliced tomatoes on top of hot buttered toast. Season with salt and pepper.

◆ Fill two slices of sourdough bread with tomato, basil and slices of buffalo mozzarella, then toast in a sandwich-maker.

◆ Top large halved tomatoes with a mixture of fresh breadcrumbs, chopped chives, parsley and oregano and olive oil before baking in the oven.

◆ Chop tomatoes into chunks and place in a salad bowl with cucumber, mild onion, freshly ground black pepper, feta and Kalamata olives. Pour a red wine vinaigrette over the top.

◆ Stir chopped tomatoes into scrambled eggs with or without sliced chorizo sausage.

◆ Chop tomatoes into chunks roughly and season well to make a delicious filling for an omelette.

◆ Combine tomato slices with sliced roasted red peppers and a vinaigrette.

◆ Fry wedges of tomato with basil leaves in butter, finish with balsamic vinegar and serve on toasted ciabatta.

ROAST RED SOUP

Roasting the ripe tomatoes and peppers makes this soup really flavoursome and sweet, as the natural sugars really develop. Garnish with fresh raw tomato for a lively effect. It will be lovely with a dry Riesling, and, for a main course, serve with toasted sandwiches.

6 large ripe beefsteak tomatoes
4 red peppers
2 red onions
2 tablespoons olive oil
1 cup red wine
2 cups chicken stock
few sprigs thyme
dash red pepper sauce (Tabasco or
　Kaitaia Fire)
pinch sugar
salt and freshly ground black pepper
1 small extra tomato, seeded and
　chopped
few basil leaves, sliced

Preheat the oven to 190°C. Slice the tomatoes and peppers in half, and cut each onion into six wedges. Place them in a large oven baking tray and sprinkle with the olive oil. Roast for about 25 minutes or until the vegetables are all soft and the edges are starting to turn dark brown. Remove from the oven and allow to cool.

Peel and discard the skins from the tomatoes and peppers. Place a sieve over a bowl, then remove and discard the seeds, taking care to catch the juice. Place the roasted tomato, pepper and onion flesh in a food processor or blender and blend until smooth. Add any juice from the bowl and return this purée to a large saucepan.

Add the wine, stock, thyme, pepper sauce and sugar, and bring to a simmer. Keep over very low heat and allow the soup to simmer for about 30 minutes, until the flavours are well blended.

Remove and discard the thyme sprigs. Season the soup to taste with salt and pepper. To serve, garnish each bowl of hot soup with tomato dice and freshly sliced basil.

SERVES 6 AS A STARTER OR MAIN COURSE

FATTOUSH

This Middle Eastern salad is good served with sliced soft goat's cheese or with pan-fried or barbecued fish fillets. If you haven't any sumac on hand, grate the zest of the lemon over the salad. Great for lunch or light supper with a glass of Pinot Gris.

6 tablespoons (90ml) olive oil, plus
    extra for shallow frying
2 rounds pita bread, split in half
1½ teaspoons sumac
3 tablespoons lemon juice
2 cloves garlic, crushed
salt and freshly ground black pepper
2 Lebanese cucumbers, halved
    lengthwise and sliced
6 tomatoes, cut into wedges
6 small radishes, thinly sliced
50g watercress, land cress or rocket
1 tablespoon torn Italian parsley,
    coriander or mint leaves

Heat a little oil in a frying pan, then fry the pita bread in batches until crisp.

Place on paper towel, sprinkle with half the sumac and leave to cool. Once cool, break into small pieces.

Whisk the oil, lemon juice and garlic together in a small bowl. Season with salt and pepper.

Place the cucumbers, tomatoes and radishes on a serving platter and spoon the dressing over them. Arrange the pita on top then the greens and herbs around the salad. Sprinkle the remaining sumac over the whole.

SERVES 6 IN A SHARED MEAL

Japanese Vegetable Rolls

This recipe is inspired by a delicious treat eaten at the Sansei Restaurant in Honolulu and Maui. Furikake, a mix of sesame seeds, dried seaweed, dried fish and salt, is available in Asian markets. As you are making the rolls, wet your hands with a little water to stop the seasoned rice sticking to your hands. Serve as starters with soy sauce, wasabi and gari (pickled ginger).

FOR THE SUSHI SU AND RICE

1 cup rice vinegar
⅔ cup sugar
2 tablespoons sea salt
1 cup short-grain rice

TO ASSEMBLE

8 mushrooms (preferably shiitake), sliced
1 red pepper, cut into quarters, then 2.5cm slices
1–2 yellow scallopini, depending on size, sliced
2 tablespoons olive oil
salt and freshly ground black pepper
4 sheets dried nori
2 cups cooked rice and 4 tablespoons sushi su (both as above, prepared as in the method)
4 tablespoons furikake (or use toasted sesame seeds)
8 slices avocado

To prepare the sushi su, put the vinegar in a small saucepan and bring to the boil over a high heat. Add the sugar and salt and stir to combine. Reduce heat to low and cook for a further five minutes.

Allow the sushi su to cool before using. This amount will season about 16 cups of cooked rice. Store in an airtight container in the refrigerator.

Place the rice in a sieve and wash under cold water until the water runs clear. Put the rice in a rice cooker. Add one cup of water and cook.

Transfer the cooked rice to a large shallow bowl. Pour four tablespoons of the sushi su into the rice. Using a rice paddle or wooden spoon, 'cut' the rice gently with a slicing motion, making sure the grains are seasoned with the sushi su. Do not over-mix or the rice will become mushy. The sushi rice is now ready to use.

To prepare the vegetables, preheat a barbecue grill or ridged griddle until hot.

In a small bowl, toss the mushrooms, red pepper and scallopini slices in the olive oil. Season with salt and pepper. Place the vegetables on the grill for two minutes per side, or until lightly browned.

(RECIPE CONTINUED ON PAGE 104)

Summer Saffron Vegetable Casserole with Rouille

This dish is almost like a bouillabaisse, but without the fish. If you serve it in an earthy casserole dish it will look superb. Make a spicy rouille (a Provençal sauce) to add to the glorious summer flavours.

750g waxy potatoes (new season's
  Agria or Nadine)
2 medium-sized bulbs fennel
500g ripe tomatoes
4–5 tablespoons extra virgin olive oil
1 medium aubergine, cut into
  6cm chunks
1 large leek, finely sliced
1 large onion, finely sliced
2 cloves garlic, finely chopped
1 teaspoon chopped thyme
½ teaspoon saffron threads
1 teaspoon salt
small pinch sugar
10cm strip orange zest
1 bay leaf
1 cup dry Chardonnay
3 tablespoons pitted black olives

For the rouille
3 cloves garlic
½ teaspoon salt
1 teaspoon cayenne or chilli powder
1 egg yolk
½ cup lighter-style olive oil

For the garnish
2 tablespoons chopped Italian parsley

To prepare the casserole, peel the potatoes and cut into wedges lengthwise. Trim the fennel, removing the scruffy leaves, and cut into wedges. Plunge the tomatoes into boiling water for 10 seconds, remove and cool in cold water, peel and cut into large chunks.

Take a large heavy pot and heat the olive oil gently. Add the potatoes, fennel, aubergine, leek and onion and cook over a low heat for a few minutes, stirring gently to coat with oil. Add the garlic, thyme, saffron, salt, sugar, orange zest and bay leaf. Continue to cook until the onion softens, then add the wine. Let it reduce by half then add the tomatoes with any juices, and water to cover (about two cups). Bring to a boil, reduce the heat and cover with a lid. Simmer until all the vegetables are tender. This should take about 25 minutes. About 10 minutes before the end of cooking, add the olives, taste for seasoning and adjust if necessary.

Meanwhile, make the rouille. Pound the garlic with the salt to form a smooth paste. Put in a small bowl and add the cayenne or chilli, working in well with the egg yolk. Gradually add the olive oil — drop by drop at first, and then whisking in constantly in a thin steady stream, until the oil is completely incorporated. Taste the rouille for seasoning and adjust if necessary. If the sauce is too thick, it can be thinned with a little hot water.

Garnish the casserole with chopped parsley and serve with the rouille.

Serves 6–8 as a main course

Zucchini and Tomato Salad

This colourful dish uses the best of the summer produce. We think it is best prepared an hour or two ahead to allow the flavours to mingle.

700g zucchini, sliced into rounds
salt
3 tablespoons olive oil
2 cloves garlic, thinly sliced
½ cup basil leaves
2 tomatoes, peeled, seeded and diced
½ lemon, juice only

Sprinkle the zucchini with salt and drain in a colander for 30 minutes. Squeeze out any liquid. Heat the oil in a frying pan and fry the zucchini until lightly coloured and soft, five to ten minutes. Add the garlic and basil, and fry for a minute more.

Toss in the tomatoes and the lemon juice, adjust the seasonings if necessary and place on a serving platter. Serve at room temperature.

Serves 6 as a side dish

Zucchini Gratin

This is a lovely baked vegetable dish and can be the perfect accompaniment to roast meat, as the clean flavours of the zucchini cut through the richness of the roast. Set them down in neat lines, topped with breadcrumbs and a little Gruyère. Choose an attractive gratin dish so it can go straight to the table after baking.

1kg small zucchini
60g butter
1 onion, finely chopped
1 tablespoon flour
250ml milk
salt and freshly ground black pepper
3–4 tablespoons finely chopped parsley
¼ cup grated Gruyère and/or
  Parmigiano Reggiano
½ cup fresh white breadcrumbs
extra knobs of butter for baking

Preheat the oven to 180°C. Slice the zucchini very neatly into four or five diagonal slices each, discarding the stalky ends. Arrange the slices in neat overlapping rows in an ovenproof serving dish.

In a heavy frying pan, melt the butter and add the chopped onion, cooking over very low heat until it is soft and starting to turn golden. Add the flour, and continue to cook for three or four minutes, stirring frequently.

Add the milk and stir well until the sauce comes to the boil. Simmer over a very low heat for seven or eight minutes, then season to taste. Add the parsley and pour the sauce over the zucchini.

Mix the cheese and breadcrumbs together and sprinkle over the surface, adding a few extra knobs of butter to keep the gratin moist. Bake in the oven for 35 or 40 minutes, until golden.

SERVES 6–8 AS A DINNER SIDE DISH, OR IN A MEAT-FREE LUNCH

Zucchini Strips with Parsley and Olives

Even people who are fussy about eating zucchini will love this way of preparation. The vegetables remain slightly crisp, and gain plenty of flavour from the garnish.

6 firm zucchini, each cut into
  5–6 strips lengthwise
3 tablespoons olive oil
3 tablespoons pitted black olives,
  lightly chopped
½ cup Italian parsley
1 lemon, zest and juice
½ teaspoon freshly ground
  black pepper

Blanch the zucchini strips in boiling salted water for one minute. Refresh under running cold water, and pat dry.

Heat the olive oil in a wide pan and toss the zucchini strips well in the oil. Add the olives, parsley, lemon zest and juice, and black pepper, tossing together briefly over the heat before turning out into a serving bowl. Serve immediately.

Serves 6–8 as a side dish

Sautéed and Steamed Zucchini

Sautéing then steaming zucchini concentrates its delicate flavour and makes a soft silky mash. It is very good as a side dish for fish or chicken, served as topping on crostini or tossed through pasta (in which case you may like to add a little ricotta or Parmigiano Reggiano).

5 tablespoons (75 ml) extra virgin olive oil
1kg zucchini, thinly sliced
2 teaspoons sea salt
4 cloves garlic, thinly sliced
⅛ teaspoon chilli flakes
small handful mint leaves, roughly chopped
small handful basil leaves, roughly chopped
1 fresh red chilli, seeded and thinly sliced

In a wide saucepan, heat the oil, add the zucchini and the sea salt.

Cook on a moderately high heat until the zucchini begins to soften, then add the garlic and the chilli flakes. Continue to cook until the zucchini begins to catch the bottom of the saucepan.

Add the mint and basil, cook for a minute, then add 100ml water and cover.

Turn the heat to low and cook for a further 10 minutes, adding a little more water if necessary. The zucchini should be soft and silky.

Adjust the seasonings and stir through the chilli slices. Serve hot or cold on bruschetta or crostini.

Serves 6 as a side dish

GRATIN OF STUFFED ZUCCHINI

This is a great way to use up that oversupply of homegrown zucchini — they all seem to come on at once. It's an easy lunch dish or you can serve it as a vegetable with a slow-roasted leg of lamb.

6 large zucchini
extra virgin olive oil
250g mascarpone
1 cup fresh breadcrumbs
2 eggs plus 2 egg yolks, lightly beaten
1 cup grated Parmigiano Reggiano
4 tablespoons chopped chervil
4 tablespoons pine nuts, toasted
salt and freshly ground black pepper
2 cups homemade tomato sauce or
 passata di pomodoro

Preheat the oven to 180°C.

Top and tail the zucchini and cut them in half lengthwise. Scoop out the seeds and discard, leaving a cavity for the filling. Lightly oil a large gratin dish and place the zucchini in it, slightly apart.

Mix together the mascarpone, breadcrumbs, eggs and egg yolks, half the Parmigiano Reggiano, all the chervil and the pine nuts. Season well with salt and pepper. Fill the zucchini with the mascarpone mixture.

Pour the passata di pomodoro around the zucchini (not over the top), then sprinkle the remaining Parmigiano Reggiano over all. Drizzle a little extra virgin olive oil over the top.

Place in the oven and cook for 20 minutes until the filling is puffed and golden and the zucchini are tender to the bite. Serve hot from the gratin dish.

SERVES 6 AS A SIDE DISH

Basil Mayonnaise

Mayonnaise made by hand has a sublime texture that mayonnaise made in a food processor cannot match. Pounding the basil creates uneven flecks, while hand-whisking produces a stiffer and more airy mayonnaise. If you prefer a milder mayonnaise, substitute a light vegetable oil for half or all of the olive oil. Delicious as an accompaniment to roasted or grilled vegetables, this mayonnaise is also very good with salmon.

½ cup firmly packed basil leaves
1 small clove garlic
sea salt
1 lemon, juice only
2 egg yolks
250ml extra virgin olive oil

Pound the basil leaves in a mortar with the garlic and a little sea salt until you have a smooth paste. Add a little lemon juice (about a teaspoon) to stop the basil from discolouring. Place in a large bowl and whisk in the egg yolks until creamy.

Add the oil drop by drop, whisking the entire time, until the eggs and oil start to emulsify, becoming thick and creamy. Then you can start adding the oil in a stream until all the oil is incorporated. The mayonnaise should be very thick. Add a little more lemon juice if needed and season to taste. If you prefer a runnier mayonnaise, add a little water to thin it down.

Alternatively, you can make the mayonnaise in a food processor. Place the basil and garlic in a food processor and chop. Add a little sea salt and the egg yolks, then gradually add the oil in a slow, steady stream. Add lemon juice to taste. Loosen and thin down the mayonnaise with a little water if necessary.

Mayonnaise keeps for about a week in the refrigerator.

Makes approximately 1½ cups

OTHER TYPES OF MAYONNAISE

Use the basic recipe on page 114, minus the garlic and basil, and add the following:

AIOLI (A GARLIC MAYONNAISE): use four cloves of garlic in the mayonnaise. For a mellower version, roast a head of garlic first and, when cool enough to handle, squeeze out the garlic pulp to use in the mixture.

SAFFRON: soak a good pinch of saffron in boiling water (a couple of tablespoons) for 20 minutes. Make the mayonnaise until you have added half the oil, then add the saffron and continue with the recipe.

WASABI: add a couple of teaspoons of wasabi paste (1 teaspoon wasabi powder), along with the garlic, to the basic mayonnaise. If you like a more fiery mayonnaise you may want to increase the amount of wasabi.

CAPER: add four tablespoons of finely chopped capers to the finished mayonnaise.

HARISSA: add two teaspoons of harissa to the finished mayonnaise (or more if you prefer your mayonnaise to have a real kick).

PEA SALSA

Bright green and bursting with flavour, this is the essence of early summer. If you have fresh peas, substitute them for the frozen. If you are using baby peas, you may need a little less sugar. Serve on crostini or bruschetta, alongside a grilled lamb chop or loosen with a little water and mix through pasta, adding ricotta and Parmigiano Reggiano to serve.

2 cloves garlic
2 cups frozen peas
¼ cup mint leaves
¼ cup basil leaves
1 teaspoon caster sugar
2 tablespoons lemon juice
¼ cup extra virgin olive oil
sea salt

Bring a pot of water to the boil. Peel the garlic cloves, add them whole and boil for five minutes. Add the peas and blanch for one minute. Drain and refresh in cold water.

Put the peas, garlic, mint and basil in a food processor and blend roughly. Add the caster sugar, lemon juice and olive oil. Blend to a chunky consistency. Season with salt to taste.

MAKES 1½ CUPS

AUTUMN

IN SEASON: Asian Greens, Aubergines, Carrots, Celeriac, Figs, Mushrooms, Onions, Peppers, Potatoes, Pumpkin, Shallots, Spinach, Witloof . . .

ASIAN GREENS

It is easy to be overwhelmed by the variety of Asian vegetables but it is good to know that Asian greens respond well to cooking in a moist heat — they love it hot and steamy. Ingredients that go well with them include ginger, garlic, chilli, spring onion, soy sauce, fish sauce, oyster sauce, fermented black beans, rice wine and sherry. Add fish and meats such as scallops, prawns, chicken, duck and roast pork. Serve these wok vegetables with rice.

BOK CHOY WITH BLACK BEANS AND GARLIC

Bok choy is Chinese white cabbage, also known as bak choi, baak choi and pak choi. Choy is the Chinese word for any leafy vegetable.

4 whole bok choy
1 tablespoon vegetable oil
2 cloves garlic, crushed
1 tablespoon fermented black beans, rinsed and roughly chopped
good pinch sugar

Cook the bok choy in a steamer, or in boiling salted water for one to two minutes. Cut in half lengthwise.

Heat the oil in a wok and stir-fry the garlic and black beans for 30 seconds.

Add the bok choy and toss to coat. Sprinkle the sugar and four tablespoons of water over the top and mix well. When hot, place in a dish and serve.

SERVES 4 AS A SIDE DISH

BABY BOK CHOY WITH GINGER AND SESAME

4 whole baby bok choy
1 tablespoon vegetable oil
1 tablespoon peeled and shredded ginger
1 clove garlic, crushed
2 teaspoons toasted sesame oil
1 tablespoon soy sauce

Cook the baby bok choy in a steamer, or in boiling salted water for one minute. If boiling, drain it well to avoid diluting any sauce.

Heat the vegetable oil in a wok and stir-fry the ginger and garlic for one minute. Add the baby bok choy and toss to coat. When hot, stir in the sesame oil and soy sauce.

Place in a serving dish and serve hot.

SERVES 4 AS A SIDE DISH

(RECIPES CONTINUED ON PAGE 120)

Penne with Aubergine, Tomato, Buffalo Mozzarella and Fresh Herbs

Salting aubergine helps to draw out any bitterness and excess moisture, which in turn prevents the aubergine from soaking up excess oil during cooking. Aubergine can be cooked on a hot grill rather than in the oven. Choose a good quality prepared tomato sauce, such as passata di pomodoro for this recipe.

1 aubergine
salt and freshly ground black pepper
8 tablespoons (120ml) extra virgin
    olive oil
2 sprigs oregano
2 cloves garlic, finely sliced
1 small red chilli, seeded and finely
    chopped
1 cup prepared tomato sauce
400g dried penne
small handful fresh basil leaves, torn
large ball (250g) buffalo mozzarella,
    torn into 4 pieces
freshly ground black pepper

Cut the aubergine into bite-sized pieces, place in a large colander and sprinkle with salt. Set aside for one hour.

Preheat the oven to 220°C.

With paper towels, wipe the moisture from the aubergine cubes and place in a shallow baking tray. Drizzle half the oil over the cubes and toss well to coat. Remove the stems from the oregano and sprinkle the leaves over the top. Place in the oven and roast for 15 to 20 minutes. Alternatively, cook on a hot grill.

To prepare the sauce, heat the remaining oil in a saucepan. Add the garlic and chilli and cook for one minute to release the flavours, taking care not to allow the garlic to brown and turn bitter. Add the tomato sauce and cook for five minutes.

Meanwhile, cook the pasta in boiling water until al dente. Drain and toss with the hot sauce. Toss through the aubergine with half the basil leaves.

Place in a large serving dish and scatter the remaining basil leaves over the top.

To serve, place the torn pieces of mozzarella around the pasta and grind over black pepper.

Serves 4 as a main course

Baked Sliced Aubergines with Cheese and Tomato

Prepare this dish ahead and pop it in the oven half an hour before serving dinner. It is really important to fry the aubergines before arranging them in the dish, so they are tender and sweet. The dish is great as a main or as a vegetable dish to accompany roast lamb.

2 large aubergines
½ cup light olive oil
300g melting cheese (havarti, raclette or Gruyère)

For the tomato sauce
pinch saffron
2 tablespoons extra virgin olive oil
2 large onions, very finely chopped
2 cloves garlic, peeled and crushed
500ml passata di pomodoro or 450g canned Italian tomatoes
½ cup water or chicken stock
pinch sugar
small bunch basil leaves
several sprigs thyme
salt and freshly ground black pepper

Cut the aubergines lengthwise into quarters and then cut into slices about 2cm thick. Heat a large frying pan and add half of the light olive oil. Add half the aubergines and fry quickly so they become golden brown on both sides. Remove and repeat this with a second batch, using the remaining light oil. Keep aside.

Cut the cheese into slices about 1cm thick and cut again to match the aubergine slices. Set aside.

To make the tomato sauce, soak the saffron in two tablespoons of boiling water. Heat a large deep pan and add the extra virgin olive oil. When hot, add the onions with the garlic, the saffron and steeping liquid, then fry gently until the onions are golden and starting to brown. Add the tomato passata (or mash the canned tomatoes, then add), the water or chicken stock and stir well. Add the sugar, herbs, salt and pepper and bring to a simmer, cooking very gently for about 20 minutes.

Remove from the heat and pass the sauce through a mouli or food processor. It should be fairly liquid, so if it is too stiff, add a little extra water. Taste to ensure it is full of flavour and adjust the seasoning if necessary.

To assemble, take an ovenproof serving dish (approximately 30cm by 20cm), and grease with a little extra olive oil. Layer the aubergine and cheese slices alternately down the dish. Spoon the sauce over the slices so they are completely bathed in tomato. Cover with foil or plastic wrap (to prevent the dish drying out or picking up other flavours) and refrigerate for later.

Remove the dish from the refrigerator about one hour before serving time so it returns to room temperature. Preheat the oven to 180°C.

Place the dish in the oven and allow to cook for 30 minutes or until it is bubbling and hot. Allow to stand for three or four minutes, then serve on heated plates.

SERVES 4–6 AS A MAIN COURSE

CANNELLINI BEAN SMASH WITH ROCKET

This delicious side dish goes well with most meats and fish. The bitterness of the rocket counters the creaminess of the cannellini beans. You could just as easily use borlotti or other dried beans, and the greens could be varied too — try watercress or blanched spinach. Alternatively, use some herbs as well as the rocket: sorrel, chives, Italian parsley and coriander would all work well.

1½ cups dried cannellini beans,
   soaked overnight (or use 2 x 400g cans)
1 stalk celery, halved
1 head garlic, halved horizontally
   (or 4 cloves, for canned beans)
salt and freshly ground black pepper
100g rocket leaves

Drain the soaked beans and rinse (or see last paragraph for canned beans). Place in a medium-sized saucepan, cover with fresh water and bring to the boil over a medium heat. Skim any foam from the surface, then add the celery and garlic. Simmer very gently for two to three hours or until tender. Drain and reserve the cooking water.

Remove and discard the celery. Squeeze the soft garlic flesh from each half of the head and add to the beans. Purée a quarter of the beans until smooth, adding a little of the reserved cooking water if necessary. Return to the bean mixture.

When ready to serve, reheat gently, thinning if necessary. Season with salt and pepper. Coarsely chop the rocket and stir through at the last minute.

Note: if you are using canned beans, drain and rinse them, cover with water, add 4 cloves of garlic and cook gently for 10 minutes. Then proceed with puréeing the beans, celery and garlic as above.

SERVES 4 AS A SIDE DISH

GINGERED CARROTS, WHITE BEANS, GREEN BEANS AND HERBS

This is a lovely fresh bright vegetable accompaniment to a roast or grilled dinner. Simplicity is everything here.

4 large carrots, peeled and cut into
  small diagonal slices
5cm piece ginger, finely chopped
knob butter
2 cups vegetable or chicken stock
300g small French beans, tops removed
1 cup preserved Italian white beans,
  well drained
3 tablespoons chopped parsley
  and mint

Put the carrots in a saucepan with the ginger, butter and stock and bring to the boil. Allow to cook for 12 to 15 minutes at a steady simmer, until all the juices are reduced and absorbed, and the carrots are tender.

Meanwhile, in a second saucepan, or in a steamer set above the carrots, cook the beans until tender. This should take only three or four minutes.

To serve, toss the carrots and green beans with the drained white beans, place on a warmed plate and scatter the herbs over the top.

SERVES 6 AS A SIDE DISH

Carrot and Celeriac Matchsticks in Herb Mayonnaise

Use this to make sandwiches, as in the photograph, or serve with bread and cold meats or seared tuna for lunch. Try kohlrabi instead of celeriac: it will add a nutty flavour and is not unlike turnip but a bit milder.

For the mayonnaise
3 egg yolks
1 teaspoon Dijon mustard
250ml pure olive oil
lemon juice, to taste
salt and freshly ground black pepper

For the salad
3 medium-sized carrots
1 lemon, juice
1 corm celeriac
1 small red onion, thinly sliced
2–3 tablespoons chopped herbs,
  such as Italian parsley and chives
½ 280g jar grilled artichokes in oil,
  optional

Place the egg yolks and mustard in the bowl of a small food processor. Process until combined, then very slowly drizzle in the olive oil. (Alternatively, make the mayonnaise by hand, using a bowl and whisk or wooden spoon.)

Add lemon juice if the mixture is becoming too thick. Season with salt and pepper and more lemon juice. Cover well and place in the refrigerator until ready to use.

Note: if your mayonnaise curdles, start again with the egg yolks and, once you have a thick mayonnaise, slowly add in the curdled mixture.

To prepare the matchsticks, peel the carrots and use a sharp knife or mandolin to cut and slice into matchsticks or julienne strips. Prepare some acidulated water — juice of a lemon added to water — to prevent the celeriac discolouring then peel the celeriac and cut into matchsticks or julienne strips, quickly placing them in the water as you cut.

Drain the julienne of celeriac and dry well, then mix with the julienne of carrots and onion slices. Add enough mayonnaise to coat the vegetables well, then mix in the chopped herbs. Drain the grilled artichokes, if using. Slice and fold through the mixture.

Keep the matchsticks and mayonnaise refrigerated, covered well, until ready to use. The mixture will keep for about a week.

Serves 6

MARINATED VEGETABLES

These quickly marinated vegetables — baby carrots, mushrooms and aubergine — all use the same basic marinade and all rely on the heat from cooking to impart flavour, but the herbs and cooking methods vary. You can prepare these a day ahead then bring them up to room temperature to serve as part of an antipasto platter, but they taste best when made on the day. It is essential to use a good-quality red wine vinegar.

MARINATED AUBERGINE

1 large aubergine
salt
¼ cup fresh basil leaves
1 tablespoon red wine vinegar
2 tablespoons extra virgin olive oil

Quarter the aubergine lengthwise and cut into small slices. Sprinkle with salt and leave to drain in a colander for an hour (this removes the excess moisture and softens the texture of the aubergine).

Squeeze out any liquid from the aubergine, then blanch in boiling water for one to two minutes, until tender. Drain, then, while still hot, place in a clean tea towel and squeeze out as much water as you can. Place in a bowl with the remaining ingredients and toss gently.

SERVES 4–6 AS A STARTER

MARINATED BABY CARROTS

250g baby carrots, scrubbed
salt and freshly ground black pepper
1 teaspoon thyme leaves, finely
  chopped
1 tablespoon red wine vinegar
2 tablespoons extra virgin olive oil

Blanch the carrots in boiling salted water until just tender.
Drain and, while still warm, mix with the remaining
ingredients. Season with salt and pepper to taste.

SERVES 4–6 AS A STARTER

MARINATED MUSHROOMS

Use small white mushrooms with tightly closed gills for this.

2 tablespoons olive oil
400g button mushrooms, trimmed
  and wiped clean
salt
1 tablespoon marjoram leaves
1 tablespoon red wine vinegar
1 tablespoon extra virgin olive oil

Heat the oil in a frying pan, add the mushrooms, season
with salt and fry for five minutes until brown and tender.
Add the marjoram and fry for another minute, then place
in a bowl with the red wine vinegar and extra virgin olive
oil and toss gently.

SERVES 4–6 AS A STARTER

RIBOLLITA

This classic Tuscan peasant soup is typically made with leftovers, available vegetables, beans and the unsalted sourdough bread of the region, used when stale. A small piece of pancetta or prosciutto bone may be added, but it isn't essential. Ribollita, meaning 'reboiled', is almost always made in large batches and the leftovers reheated for the next day, without adding stock. Calling it a soup is a bit of a misnomer — there is usually little liquid, making it more stew-like.

1 cup dried beans (cannellini or
   borlotti) soaked overnight in
   cold water
aromatic vegetables such as tomato,
   celery, sage sprigs and garlic, for the
   soup base
2 tablespoons olive oil
2 medium-sized onions, finely chopped
2 carrots, peeled and coarsely chopped
1 stalk celery, coarsely chopped
bunch of greens, such as silver beet
   (not a coloured variety), cavolo nero,
   spinach or Savoy cabbage
handful sage leaves, finely chopped
3 cloves garlic, chopped
2 cups day-old sourdough bread, broken
   into small chunks
3 tablespoons Italian parsley,
   coarsely chopped
salt and freshly ground black pepper
extra virgin olive oil for drizzling
grated Parmigiano Reggiano
   for serving

Drain the beans and discard the soaking water. Place in a saucepan, cover with cold water and add the aromatic vegetables. Remove the froth that forms on top of the water as it comes to the boil.

Simmer slowly, uncovered, until the beans are tender (one to two hours). Remove the aromatics (although we often mash up the tomato and garlic, and put them back in with the beans). Drain and reserve the cooking water. Purée half the beans with some of the cooking water and set aside.

Heat the oil in a large saucepan and sauté the chopped onions, carrots and celery for 15 minutes. If using silver beet as a green, remove and chop the stems, blanch these and add them to the sauté mixture to cook for a few minutes. Add the sage and garlic and cook for another 15 minutes.

In a separate saucepan, blanch the remaining greens (including silver beet leaves) in boiling salted water until tender. Squeeze out any excess water and chop coarsely.

Pour the reserved cooking water into the saucepan, adding stock or water if necessary to make it up to three cups. Add the whole beans and simmer for 30 minutes.

Add the blanched green leaves, bean purée and sourdough. Simmer for a few minutes, then add the parsley. Season with salt and pepper.

Serve in warm bowls with a drizzle of a peppery extra virgin olive oil and Parmigiano Reggiano.

SERVES 6–8 AS A STARTER

BRAISED CHICKPEAS WITH CRISPY ONIONS AND MOJO VERDE

This makes a fine vegetarian meal, full of spice and texture. Leave out the haloumi and it's a very good accompaniment to simple pan-fried lamb steaks. If you choose dried chickpeas, check they are not heat-treated before you buy them.

FOR THE MOJO VERDE
3 cloves garlic
1 teaspoon cumin seeds, toasted
 and ground
1 teaspoon sea salt
½ cup tightly packed coriander leaves
2 tablespoons sherry or white wine
 vinegar
4 tablespoons olive oil

FOR THE CRISPY ONIONS
2 cups oil for frying (we used rice
 bran oil)
2 onions, thinly sliced into rounds

FOR THE BRAISED CHICKPEAS
1½ cups dried chickpeas, soaked
 overnight (or 2 x 400g cans,
 drained and rinsed)
2 tablespoons olive oil
2 medium-sized onions, finely chopped
4 cloves garlic, finely chopped (plus
 extra for cooking the chickpeas)
3 small dried chillies, crumbled (plus
 extra for cooking the chickpeas)
2 teaspoons ground cumin
2 tablespoons tomato paste
400g spinach leaves (stems discarded),
 blanched and coarsely chopped
sea salt and freshly ground
 black pepper
400g haloumi, cut into 5mm slices
extra olive oil for the haloumi

To make the mojo verde, place the garlic, cumin and sea salt in a food processor and process until smooth. Add the coriander, vinegar and olive oil. Process until emulsified. The dressing should be quite vinegary.

To prepare the crispy onions, place the oil and onions in a saucepan and slowly bring to the boil. Cook until the onions turn golden, about 20 minutes.

Drain the onions on paper towels (they will become crisp as they cool). If not using immediately, store in an airtight container between layers of paper towels for up to two days. The onions can be re-crisped in the oven if necessary.

If using soaked chickpeas, drain them and place in a saucepan of unsalted water with the extra garlic and chilli for added flavour. Simmer until tender, one to two hours. When ready, discard the garlic and chilli, but reserve the cooking water.

In a medium-sized saucepan, heat the oil and fry the onions until soft but not coloured, about 10 minutes. Add the garlic, chillies and cumin, and fry for a few more minutes. Mix in the tomato paste, then add the chickpeas, stirring well to coat.

Add two cups of the reserved cooking liquid, or water if using canned chickpeas, and cook until most of the liquid has disappeared. Add the spinach, stir well to combine and cook until heated through. Season to taste.

Pan-fry the haloumi slices over a medium heat with a little extra olive oil. Cook until golden, about one minute each side.

To serve, place a spoonful of braised chickpeas in each bowl. Add a few slices of warm haloumi, drizzle the mojo verde over, and top with the crispy onions.

SERVES 4 AS A MAIN COURSE

PERFECT ROAST POTATOES

Cooks who have perfected the art of roast potatoes will find that family, friends and visitors will demand them constantly. Choosing the right potato is important, as you want a crisp crunchy exterior and a light fluffy interior. Our favourite is Agria, which have a beautiful flavour too — perfect with roast or grilled meat or chicken.

1kg floury potatoes (Agria, Desiree, Red Rascal)
3–4 tablespoons olive oil
2 tablespoons butter
salt and freshly ground black pepper

Preheat the oven to 190°C.

Peel the potatoes and cut into neatly shaped, evenly sized chunks or wedges about 7cm or 8cm in diameter. Place in a saucepan of salted water and bring to a simmer. Allow to simmer for four to five minutes.

Drain well so the potatoes are completely dry, then score the surface of each potato with a fork, to rough it up a little.

Take a heavy oven baking dish, tip in the oil and then the butter. Place in the oven so that the butter melts and the oil heats up.

Add the scored potatoes, tossing well so that every surface is covered with the oil and butter mixture, and adding plenty of salt and pepper.

Roast for an hour, or until the potatoes are crisp and golden. Serve at once.

SERVES 6 AS A SIDE DISH

AUTUMN MEANS . . . POTATOES

Potatoes are everyone's favourite. There is no distinct season for this versatile vegetable as potatoes appear year round, but as the weather cools the potato appeals as a key ingredient in many dishes. It has become a staple ingredient in the Western diet and provides a wealth of nutrients, especially vitamin C and potassium. If there's a potato in the store cupboard, there's a delicious meal in the house. And despite some claims, potatoes are not fattening, though some cooking and preparation methods may be.

ALL ABOUT POTATOES

POTATO VARIETIES

Each of the many varieties of potato grown has its own special characteristics. Potatoes can be divided into three groups, and should be labelled well in supermarkets and green grocers' stores.

WAXY potatoes are mostly the 'early' new-season varieties. They are ideal for boiling, salads, casseroles and soups. Varieties include Draga, Victoria, Frisia, Jersey Bennes, Liseta, Red King, Tiffany and Nadine.

FLOURY potatoes are the ones that crumble a little in the cooking process and are ideal for mashing, wedges, roasting, chips and baking. Look for Ilam Hardy, Red Rascal, Agria, White Delight and Fianna.

GENERAL-PURPOSE potatoes are neither distinctly waxy nor floury and are suitable for most uses and cooking methods. Rua, Desiree, Moonlight, Rocket, Maris Anchor and Karaka are general-purpose varieties. Note that as the season for potatoes progresses, they change, and such factors as weather, climate and soil can affect the texture and flavour.

STORING POTATOES

Don't wash potatoes before storing, as the natural dirt and dust helps them to keep fresher.

Potatoes keep best when stored in a cool dark place, removed from their plastic bags. A heavy paper bag or cardboard box makes a great storage container.

When stored in temperatures higher than 7°C, they tend to sprout — and if kept too cold their starch will turn to sugar, so avoid storing potatoes in the refrigerator.

Potatoes exposed to light can develop a green colour, which is due to chlorophyll formation in the surface layers. New potatoes (meaning freshly dug potatoes) are particularly susceptible to this. Cut off any green pieces before cooking your potatoes.

QUICK WAYS WITH POTATOES

MASHED POTATOES: The secret to mashing potatoes is to drain them well after boiling and then whip with a knob of butter in heated milk that is at simmering point, beating all the while with a masher or wooden spoon (or a potato ricer or mouli, to more easily obtain a lump-free mash). Floury potatoes are essential for a great result. Added flavourings for mashed spuds include:

- wasabi or horseradish
- grated cheddar cheese
- other melting cheeses
- chopped parsley
- chopped coriander
- crushed garlic
- Indian spices
- pesto
- harissa
- chopped spring onions
- lemon zest
- chopped anchovy fillets
- crispy bacon lardons
- olive oil and chopped pitted olives

BAKED POTATOES: Bake large floury potatoes, well scrubbed and stabbed with a fork to prevent exploding, in a hot oven for an hour. Allow to cool, scoop out the flesh, mash well with any of the above flavourings (or a combination of them) and return the mixture to the potato shells. Sprinkle with olive oil or butter, return to the oven and bake for about 15 minutes, until well browned.

SOUPS AND CURRIES: Potatoes are wonderful for thickening soups and curries. Add small cubes to the soup or curry while it is cooking, and after long slow simmering the potato melts into the liquid and provides a thickened result.

STEAMED POTATOES: Choose a waxy style of potato for steaming. When the potatoes are tender, toss in butter and chopped parsley for a traditional accompaniment for any fish dish. Steamed potatoes are great in potato salads. Dress potatoes while still warm with oil, vinegar and seasoning. Add green beans and black olives.

PIE TOPPINGS: Potatoes make a great change to the more conventional topping of pastry for any pie. Cook potatoes until tender, mash well and pipe over fish, meat or chicken pies. Dot with butter or cheese to ensure the topping is golden brown.

COCKTAIL FOOD: The tiny new-season Jersey Bennes, which first appear in late spring, make a great cocktail idea. Boil or steam them, carefully cut in half and serve with:

- a dollop of tasty pesto

- flavoured sour cream

- ham julienne

- sour cream and fish roe, topped with chervil

- smoked salmon and mayonnaise.

SAUTÉED POTATOES: Use left-over cooked floury potatoes, cut into chunky pieces. Sauté in oil (or, even better, use duck fat), tossing until the pieces are golden and crusty. This takes up to 15 to 20 minutes. You can add mushrooms and a handful of chopped parsley for a luxurious bubble and squeak.

FRITTATA: Mix cooked potatoes with spinach and herbs, then fry them slowly with beaten eggs in an omelette pan. This makes a wonderfully filling frittata.

Baked Potatoes with Porcini

This is a wonderfully aromatic dish that requires a little preparation but looks after itself once it is in the oven. The porcini give it a real dollop of flavour, though you could leave them out and substitute lots of extra thyme.

15g dried porcini mushrooms
1.5kg waxy or general-purpose potatoes
100g butter, melted
6–8 thyme sprigs, chopped
salt and freshly ground black pepper
2 cups chicken or vegetable stock
extra thyme for topping

Soak the dried porcini in enough boiling water to just cover them. Leave for at least 30 minutes. Preheat the oven to 200°C.

Use a little of the butter to grease an ovenproof dish. Peel the potatoes and slice them thinly, preferably with a mandolin. Drain the porcini and chop finely.

Make a layer of the potatoes in the dish, then scatter a third of the porcini over them with a little thyme, salt and pepper. Continue to layer the potatoes in the dish, adding porcini, thyme and salt and pepper to each layer.

Heat the stock with the remaining butter and pour this carefully into the dish. Add black pepper and a little extra thyme to the top if desired.

Bake for about one hour so that the potatoes are golden and crisp and the chicken stock has been thoroughly absorbed. Serve at once.

Serves 6–8 as a side dish

Sweet and Sour Roasted Pumpkin

Sweet and sour combinations are a favourite. This is a very pretty dish of orange and pink colours, with golden raisins complementing the colours. However, ordinary raisins are fine to use instead. Pomegranate molasses is found in specialist food stores and some supermarkets.

3 tablespoons golden raisins
3 tablespoons sherry or water
2 tablespoons red wine vinegar
2 tablespoons sugar
¼ cup water
1 small red onion, thinly sliced
1 clove garlic
½ teaspoon sea salt
2 tablespoons pomegranate molasses
2 tablespoons extra virgin olive oil
½ medium-sized pumpkin (approx 800g with skin and seeds removed), peeled and cut into thin slices

Preheat the oven to 200°C. Soak the raisins in the sherry or water and set aside for 20 minutes.

Place the red wine vinegar, sugar and the water in a saucepan and bring to the boil. When the sugar has dissolved, pour the liquid over the red onion to pickle it. Set aside for 30 minutes.

Crush the garlic to a paste with the salt, using the side of your knife. Place in a large bowl with the pomegranate molasses and olive oil, and mix together. Add the pumpkin and toss it in this marinade to coat the pieces.

Lay the pumpkin pieces flat on a baking tray and bake for 30 minutes, or until the pumpkin is cooked.

To serve, place the pumpkin pieces on a platter, distribute the onions over them and scatter the raisins over the top.

Serves 6–8 as a side dish

Oven-Baked Pumpkin with Basil Parsley Sauce

An easy-to-prepare pumpkin dish that can cook in the oven beside roasting lamb. Keep the basil parsley sauce well covered or the surface will discolour.

750g pumpkin, peeled and cubed
245ml olive oil
salt and freshly ground black pepper
2 cups homemade tomato sauce or
   bottled passata di pomodoro
2 well-packed cups basil
½ cup parsley
1 clove garlic, crushed
1 tablespoon lemon juice
extra salt and freshly ground black
   pepper, for the sauce

Preheat the oven to 180°C.

In an oven dish with a tight-fitting lid, toss the pumpkin with three tablespoons of the oil, salt and pepper. Stir the tomato sauce through this.

Bake, covered, for 45 minutes or until the pumpkin is soft. Stir once or twice during cooking.

To make the sauce, process the herbs, garlic, salt and pepper in a food processor until the herbs are well chopped. Add the lemon, drizzle in 200ml of the oil and blend to combine. Season to taste.

Place the sauce in a small bowl, cover well with plastic wrap and store in the refrigerator until needed.

To serve, drizzle the hot cooked pumpkin with the basil parsley sauce.

SERVES 6 AS A SIDE DISH

TOMATO, RICE AND ORANGE SOUP

This delicious recipe is inspired by Lindsey Bareham's recipe in *The Big Red Book of Tomatoes*. You can make the soup ahead, but don't add the rice until just before you plan on serving it, as the rice continues to swell and thicken the soup, giving it an almost risotto-like quality. If you prefer a thinner soup, use half the amount of rice in the recipe.

2 tablespoons olive oil
1 large onion, finely chopped
2 cloves garlic, finely chopped
2 teaspoons coriander seeds, toasted
  and ground
1 orange, zest and juice
2 x 400g cans tomatoes, mashed
3 cups vegetable stock or water
1 teaspoon sea salt
½ cup long-grain rice
small bunch coriander, stems removed
sea salt and freshly ground
  black pepper

In a large saucepan, heat the oil and sauté the onion and garlic until soft but not coloured. Add the ground coriander and orange zest, and cook for one minute.

Add the tomatoes, vegetable stock and salt, bring to the boil then simmer for 15 minutes, using a wooden spoon to break up the tomatoes if necessary.

Stir in the rice and cook for 15 minutes or until the rice is cooked. Roughly chop the coriander leaves. Finally, add the orange juice and coriander, and season with salt and pepper to taste.

SERVES 6 AS A STARTER

Roma Tomato Upside-Down Tart

A quick tart for that last-minute lunch. Serve with a green salad and some goat's curd or very soft goat's cheese mixed with chopped fresh herbs such as mint and fennel — and grate in the zest of a lemon. To make the tart, you will need a heavy cast-iron pan with a cast iron handle, or something similar that is suitable for both stove-top and oven cooking.

1 sheet frozen pre-rolled butter
   puff pastry
5 large Roma tomatoes
1 teaspoon caster sugar
salt and freshly ground black pepper
a little olive oil
10 basil leaves, plus extra for garnish
a little milk for glazing (optional)

Thaw the pastry sheet, ensuring it is still very cold and firm for use. Preheat the oven to 200°C.

Cut the Roma tomatoes in half lengthwise, discard the cores and place in a bowl with the caster sugar. Season with salt and freshly ground black pepper.

Smear a little olive oil across the base of a heavy cast-iron frying pan (diameter about 16cm). Arrange the tomatoes in the bottom of the pan and place on the stove over a medium heat. This will allow the tomatoes to colour a little. Cook for about five minutes, or until most of the liquid from the tomatoes has reduced. Lower the heat if necessary. Place a basil leaf on top of each tomato for flavour.

Cut the cold, firm pastry sheet slightly larger than the top of the pan. Working quickly, place the pastry circle over the tomatoes and make a slit in the top to allow any steam to be released. Brush the pastry with a little milk, if using.

Bake the tart in the oven for 20 to 25 minutes, until the pastry is well browned. Leave for five minutes before turning out upside down (with the pastry on the bottom) on a large serving plate. Shred a few extra basil leaves and sprinkle over the tart before serving.

Serves 3–4 as a starter or lunch dish

TOMATO AND FENNEL SALAD

A simple salad starter — use sourdough bread to mop up the vinaigrette. The use of fennel here also makes this salad a superb combination with barbecued fish. A New Zealand Pinot Gris with plenty of body will stand up to the fennel. Slice the fennel as thinly as possible with a sharp knife or a mandolin.

6 large ripe tomatoes, thinly sliced
2 small bulbs fennel, thinly sliced and
  green fronds finely chopped
6 tablespoons (90ml) lemon-infused
  olive oil
3 tablespoons lemon juice
salt and freshly ground black pepper

Arrange the tomato and fennel slices on individual serving plates or one large platter.

Mix the green fennel fronds with the olive oil and lemon juice. Season with salt and pepper.

Spoon the dressing over the tomatoes and fennel, and set aside at room temperature for one hour before serving. Serve with a sourdough loaf.

SERVES 6 AS A STARTER

Sweet and Sour Shallots

Here shallots are roasted with a sweet and sour marinade until tender and golden. This dish is inspired by a recipe in Rosemary Barron's *Meze*. The quantity can easily be doubled and will keep for up to a week in the refrigerator. It is excellent on an antipasto platter but also delicious added to a salad of bitter greens such as rocket, radicchio, endive, witloof or watercress.

16 shallots
2 tablespoons olive oil
2 tablespoons sherry vinegar
1 tablespoon liquid honey
1 teaspoon thyme leaves
sea salt
3 tablespoons currants

Preheat the oven to 200°C. Trim the tail and stem ends of the shallots and boil in salted water for five minutes.

When cool enough to handle, remove and discard the skins. Combine the shallots with the remaining ingredients, except the currants.

Bake for 40 minutes, or until golden and tender. Add a little water if necessary to stop the shallots from drying out.

Soak the currants in boiling water for 20 minutes to soften. Drain and add to the warm shallots.

Serves 4 as a side dish

Green Salad with Grilled Pears, Fresh Figs, Roasted Almonds and Goat's Cheese

This lovely autumnal salad combines leaves, fruit and nuts with a tangy goat cheese. This salad would also be lovely with persimmon instead of pear, when in season.

3 pears
2 tablespoons light fruity olive oil
1 small cos lettuce, leaves separated
2 cups rocket leaves, stalky ends
  removed
6 small ripe figs, halved
½ cup roasted almonds
200g soft goat's cheese, chopped into
  2cm chunks

For the dressing
1 lemon, juice and zest
6 tablespoons (90 ml) fruity olive oil
1 teaspoon Dijon mustard
salt and freshly ground black pepper

To serve
handful mint leaves, roughly chopped

Peel and core the pears, quarter, then cut each quarter into three slices. Heat a grill plate until moderately hot. Lightly brush the pears with the oil and place on the heated grill plate for about two minutes each side. Remove and cool.

Break the cos leaves into bite-sized pieces and mix with the rocket leaves. Arrange these on a flat serving platter or in a shallow bowl. Place the grilled pears, the figs, almonds and goat's cheese chunks on top of the leaves.

Make the dressing by combining all the ingredients in a small jar, shaking really well to mix. Scatter the mint on the salad and drizzle the vinaigrette over the top.

Serves 6 as a starter

Vegetable and Green Lentil Soup

Keep all the vegetables the same size so they cook evenly — remember the pieces need to sit easily on a soup spoon. This is wonderful with crusty bread and butter.

1 tablespoon olive oil
1 small onion, finely sliced
1 small leek, finely sliced,
  (white part only)
2 cloves garlic, crushed
1 small red chilli, seeded and finely
  chopped
1 small carrot, cut into evenly
  sized pieces
½ small swede, peeled and cut into
  evenly sized pieces
1 stalk celery, strings removed and cut
  into evenly sized pieces
1 small bulb fennel, trimmed and very
  finely sliced
400g can Roma tomatoes in juice,
  chopped
1 litre vegetable stock
50g green Puy lentils
1 bay leaf, sprigs of fresh thyme and
  parsley, tied together
salt and freshly ground black pepper

In a large heavy-based saucepan, heat the oil over a low heat.

Place the onion and leek in the pan and cook for 10 minutes until soft. Add the garlic and chilli and cook a further two minutes, then add the carrot, swede, celery and fennel and cook for five minutes. Stir in the tomatoes and their juice, stock, lentils and herbs.

Bring to the boil, turn the heat down and simmer for 30 minutes until the vegetables and lentils are just soft. Remove the herb bundle and taste the soup for seasoning. Serve hot.

SERVES 4 GENEROUSLY AS A STARTER OR LUNCH DISH

Braised Witloof

With its crisp, lightly bitter leaves, witloof — also called chicory and Belgian or French endive — is a wonderful addition to autumn salads. When it is braised, its bitterness mellows and the sweetness develops. This makes it an excellent companion to plain grilled meats.

50g butter, extra for greasing
4 witloof, cut in half lengthwise
1 clove garlic, thinly sliced
salt and freshly ground black pepper
½ cup chicken or vegetable stock
½ cup fresh coarse breadcrumbs
40g blue cheese, crumbled

Preheat the oven to 180°C. Grease a baking dish with butter.

Heat a frying pan and add half the butter. Add the witloof, cut side down, and brown for a few minutes. Turn it over and repeat with the other side (you may need to do this in batches).

Arrange all the witloof in the baking dish — the pieces should fit quite snugly. Tuck a sliver of garlic inside each, then scatter any remaining garlic over the top. Season with salt and pepper, add the stock and cover with foil.

Bake in the oven for 20 minutes, until most of the liquid has disappeared. Scatter the breadcrumbs, blue cheese and remaining butter over the top and return to the oven for a further 20 minutes, or until the crumbs are golden. Serve hot.

Serves 4–6 as a side dish

WINTER

IN SEASON: **Broccoli, Broccolini, Brussels Sprouts, Cabbages, Carrots, Cauliflowers, Celery, Chokos, Leeks, Mushrooms, Onions, Parsnips, Potatoes, Pumpkins, Silver Beet, Spinach, Swedes, Turnips . . .**

Broccoli with Orecchiette, Chilli and Pecorino Cheese

This recipe comes from Puglia where orecchiette pasta and broccoli are often combined. When in season, substitute snow beans (300g, trimmed and thinly sliced lengthwise) for the broccoli. Delicious served with a glass of Pinot Gris from the Wairarapa and a local pecorino cheese.

500g broccoli
4 tablespoons extra virgin olive oil
400g dried orecchiette pasta
1 clove garlic, sliced
1 small red chilli, seeded and
  finely chopped
4 tomatoes, skinned, seeded
  and quartered
4–5 basil leaves
shaved pecorino

Cut the broccoli into small florets and cook in a large saucepan of lightly salted boiling water until tender, three to four minutes. Remove the broccoli, reserving the water, and drain well in a colander. Splash two tablespoons of the oil over the florets. Set aside. Bring the water back to the boil, add the orecchiette and cook until just tender, 10 to 15 minutes.

Place the remaining oil in a frying pan, add the garlic and chilli and fry gently for about one minute. Add the tomatoes and basil leaves, then the cooked broccoli.

Warm through the broccoli, then mix with the cooked pasta. Place in a large bowl and top with shaved pecorino. Serve hot.

Serves 4 for lunch

BROCCOLI PASTA

This is the simplest of recipes and makes a delicious lunch or starter. Most of the broccoli is puréed and acts as a sauce for the pasta. We used the Montebello Organic Penne Rigate pasta for this, and the addition of lemon zest from organic lemons lifted the dish to a new high.

1 cup dried penne
4 tablespoons high-quality extra
   virgin olive oil
1 large head broccoli, chopped
   (including peeled stalks)
½ lemon, grated zest
½ cup finely grated Parmigiano
   Reggiano
salt and freshly ground black pepper

Bring a saucepan of well-salted water to a rolling boil, add the penne and simmer for eight minutes. Drain, return to the pan and toss with one tablespoon of the oil.

Meanwhile, bring another pan of salted water to a simmer and add the broccoli. Simmer for six to seven minutes, until tender. Place a sieve over a bowl and drain the broccoli, catching the cooking water in the bowl.

Reserve a few of the florets and put the rest of the broccoli in the food processor. Process the broccoli until smooth, adding a few tablespoons of the broccoli cooking water. You should have a lovely liquidy sauce.

Stir in the lemon zest, two tablespoons of the oil and half the cheese. Tip this broccoli sauce over the hot pasta and stir well to coat all the pasta. Taste and adjust the seasoning with salt and pepper. Serve at once, garnished with the reserved broccoli florets and topped with a dash of olive oil. Hand the remaining cheese around.

SERVES 4 AS A STARTER

BROCCOLI WITH CHILLI AND LEMON

Vegetables such as broccoli, cauliflower, green beans and spinach can be sautéed in hot oil, garlic and chilli to enhance their flavour or to reheat them when they have already been cooked.

500g broccoli
2 tablespoons olive oil
2 cloves garlic, sliced
1 red chilli, seeded and finely sliced
salt and freshly ground black pepper
few drops lemon juice

Cut the broccoli into florets and cook in salted water or steam until bite-tender.

Place the oil in a frying pan and fry the garlic and chilli for 30 seconds. Make sure the garlic doesn't burn or it will taste bitter. Add the broccoli and stir-fry until hot.

Place in a serving bowl, season with salt and pepper and squeeze the lemon juice over the top. Serve immediately.

SERVES 4 AS A SIDE DISH

BROCCOLI AND SPINACH SOUP

Creamed vegetable soups are easy to make if you have a blender or mouli. Once the technique is mastered, the vegetable content can be varied endlessly.

700g broccoli and spinach, leaves
   and stalks chopped
1 small onion, chopped
1 small potato, peeled and chopped
2½ cups chicken or vegetable stock
1 cup cream
salt and freshly ground black pepper
olive oil for drizzling
6 lemon wedges for squeezing

Place all the broccoli and spinach in a large saucepan with the onion, potato and stock. Bring to the boil, cover and cook until the vegetables are tender.

Allow to cool a little before putting through a blender, then return the purée to the saucepan.

Add the cream, and salt and pepper to taste. Bring almost to the boiling point (but do not boil).

Pour into soup bowls and drizzle with olive oil. Serve with wedges of lemon and fresh bread.

SERVES 6 AS A STARTER

BUTTERED BRUSSELS SPROUTS

In our opinion, those who hate Brussels sprouts simply haven't had them prepared properly. They shouldn't be overcooked — that is when the objectionable sulphurous odours arise. It is important to cook them in plenty of salted water without the saucepan lid on.

600g Brussels sprouts
50g butter
sea salt and freshly ground
    black pepper
2 tablespoons chopped herbs,
    such as Italian parsley or chives

Trim off and discard the outer leaves of the Brussels sprouts. Cut a small cross in the base of each sprout (this helps to ensure that the core, which takes longer to cook, will be tender).

Cook in a pot of boiling salted water for five to ten minutes if whole (or four minutes if cut in half), then drain well. Melt the butter in a pan, add the sprouts and cook for a minute or two.

Season with salt and pepper and scatter the herbs over the top. Serve immediately.

SERVES 4 AS A SIDE DISH

BRUSSELS SPROUTS AND HAZELNUT BROWN BUTTER

The Brussels sprouts are sliced thinly, making this a quick dish to cook. It is excellent with simple grilled meats.

600g Brussels sprouts
50g butter
¼ cup water
1 lemon, juice
sea salt and freshly ground black
   pepper
¼ cup skinned toasted hazelnuts,
   roughly chopped

Trim off and discard the outer Brussels sprouts leaves. Cut each sprout in half and cut out the tiny core. Thinly slice the sprouts.

In a large sauté pan melt half the butter, add the sprouts and stir and coat in the butter. Add the water and half the lemon juice, then cook for one minute. Meanwhile, warm a serving bowl.

Season with salt and pepper and add the remaining butter, lemon juice and the hazelnuts. Combine well, then place in the warmed bowl to serve.

SERVES 4 AS A SIDE DISH

WINTER MEANS . . . GREENS: BROCCOLI, BRUSSELS SPROUTS, CABBAGES AND SILVER BEET

The green vegetables of winter are produced as strong, slower-growing plants than the greens of the other seasons. But this process gives them plenty of flavour and as a rule they have a longer keeping quality than their summer cousins.

They are often known as the 'nutritional heavyweights': they are packed with nutrients including Vitamins B, C and K, plus high calcium, iron and potassium. And like all vegetables they are best cooked and served while very fresh.

ALL ABOUT WINTER GREENS

BUYING TIPS

◆ Buy smaller quantities regularly from a reputable vegetable supplier who has a high turnover of crisp, fresh stock.

◆ Look for winter greens with bright, firm leaves.

◆ Ensure the vegetable has been harvested recently and has not dried out at the point where it was cut from the plant.

◆ Check there are no black spots and no parts of the vegetable where the green colour has started to turn yellowish.

STORING WINTER GREENS

Ethylene, a gas given off naturally by some vegetables and fruits, hastens both ripening and deterioration. As winter greens are ethylene sensitive, it's important to store cabbages, silver beet, broccoli and Brussels sprouts separately from apples, tomatoes and avocados, the fruits that produce ethylene.

The best place to store green vegetables is in the chiller compartment of the refrigerator. Make sure they are not packed in tightly: they should have plenty of air circulating through and around them.

BROCCOLI

Several varieties are available, the most common being sprouting broccoli or calabrese. But as winter draws in we also see romanesco broccoli, which has light green, almost coral-like clusters of heads. Broccolini, a cross between broccoli and the Chinese vegetable gai lan, has become popular with its small florets on long stems. And often specialist green grocers offer purple broccoli. These variations on broccoli are all highly nutritious and can be used in any recipe that calls for broccoli.

- Add to stir-fries.

- Steam and serve with cheesy sauce.

- Cook until tender, purée and mix with a little cream and Parmigiano Reggiano.

- Blanch for two minutes and add to winter salads.

- Make into a velvety soup with good stock and a few onions.

BRUSSELS SPROUTS

One of the most underrated vegetables, Brussels sprouts, with their cute mini-cabbage looks, are a tasty savoury treat. And they are far more versatile than many cooks think. Early in winter, Brussels sprouts are tiny and compact with a piquancy that comes from their high mustard oil content. Later in the season the sprouts are larger with looser leaves and a slightly sweeter flavour. Look for firm sprouts that have no spots or yellowing.

- Cut a small cross in the base of each Brussels sprout when steaming or simmering to ensure quicker cooking.

- Quarter the sprouts and add to a stir-fry with herbs or spices.

- Deconstruct the leaves and steam quickly. Serve with butter and chopped nuts.

- Finely slice each sprout, quickly sauté in olive oil and garnish with parsley.

- Finely sliced Brussels sprouts are also great in salads.

Cabbages

The most commonly grown cabbage is the green Drumhead variety with tightly packed leaves. Also available throughout winter are red cabbages, with their beautiful crimson leaves, and the crinkly, sweet Savoy cabbage.

◆ Look for cabbages that are dense and heavy, with crisp leaves. Often the outer leaves can be tough and damaged; these leaves should be discarded. Cabbage can be eaten raw or cooked but it is important to choose really fresh examples for salads and coleslaws.

◆ Avoid overcooking: this destroys its goodness and makes the flavours rather soggy.

◆ Slice fresh cabbage very finely and mix with other shredded vegetables and a tasty vinaigrette for an excellent coleslaw.

◆ Blanch cabbage leaves, then wrap them around a savoury stuffing and simmer in good stock until tender.

◆ Pickle sliced cabbage to make crunchy sauerkraut.

◆ Stir-fry cabbage in olive oil with a little onion and some caraway seeds until tender, but still slightly crisp — this makes a great side dish.

Silver beet

Also known as Swiss chard, silver beet is a terrific plant to grow in the smallest of gardens: it lasts for a far longer time before turning to seed than most leafy vegetables. It is highly nutritious and was considered a real delicacy by the ancient Romans and Greeks.
The flavour is stronger than spinach so it is best eaten when cooked, although very young leaves can be added to a salad.

◆ Look for silver beet with white stems or the rarer beet with bright pink stems.

◆ Slice and add to stir-fries.

◆ Strip the leaves off and cook in any recipe, but keep the stalks as they are really delicious when slow-cooked for a long time and served with a cheesy sauce.

◆ Simmer silver beet leaves until tender, drain well and chop. This can then fill a quiche, a pie or an omelette.

◆ Make a silver beet roulade: add finely chopped cooked silver beet to beaten eggs with a touch of nutmeg, and bake on a tray. Fill with mushrooms or cheese sauce.

◆ Silver beet goes well with lemon, nutmeg and cheese, so add any of these when steaming or simmering.

CABBAGE ROLLS IN SAVOURY BROTH

This tasty soup makes a great lunch in cooler weather. The cabbage rolls are easy to prepare as the filling is not pre-cooked. It can be prepared ahead, rolled in the cabbage leaves and refrigerated. It's important to have a strongly flavoured stock or broth for this soup — and remember to reserve the porcini liquid to add to this for further flavour. Serve with warm ciabatta bread.

FOR THE CABBAGE ROLLS

10g dried porcini

1 Savoy cabbage

1 clove garlic, crushed

200g button mushrooms,
   finely chopped

½ teaspoon freshly ground
   black pepper

several sprigs tarragon or thyme,
   stems discarded and leaves chopped

6 slices stale white bread
   (crusts discarded), crumbled

2 eggs, lightly beaten

1 teaspoon salt

FOR THE BROTH

2 litres very well-flavoured
   vegetable or chicken stock

2 tomatoes, peeled, seeded and
   chopped into strips

1 small bunch parsley, leaves
   finely chopped

To make the cabbage rolls, first soak the porcini for 30 minutes. Reserve the soaking water and chop the porcini.

Separate the leaves from the cabbage, taking care not to tear them so the leaves remain whole. Cook for four to five minutes in boiling salted water, then drain.

Mix the garlic, chopped mushrooms and porcini, pepper, herbs and bread together. Add the beaten eggs and salt, and work the mixture into a paste with your hands.

Divide the mixture into 18 pieces and shape these into cylinders. Then roll a cabbage leaf around each piece of filling and secure with a toothpick.

In a large wide pan, bring the stock to a very gentle simmer and add the reserved porcini water. Gently add the cabbage parcels and poach them for at least 15 minutes in barely simmering water. Turn them over halfway through the cooking process. Place three parcels in each serving bowl, removing the toothpicks.

Add the tomato strips and parsley to the broth, reheat and ladle the soup over the cabbage rolls. Serve immediately.

SERVES 6 AS A STARTER OR LIGHT MEAL

Cabbage with Coriander and Coconut

Simple dishes are often the most popular way with vegetables. Steaming cabbage lightly and tossing it in coconut cream and chopped coriander is an exciting use for this really versatile vegetable.

2 tablespoons light olive oil
1 small cabbage, finely sliced
salt and freshly ground black pepper
400ml can coconut cream
½ cup chopped coriander

Heat the olive oil in a heavy pan and add the cabbage. Toss well over gentle heat until it begins to soften, three to four minutes.

Add salt, pepper and the coconut cream and allow the cabbage to come to a simmer. Simmer for about two minutes, tip in the coriander and serve at once.

SERVES 6 AS A SIDE DISH

Winter Coleslaw

Don't hold back: all sorts of crunchy winter vegetables can be finely sliced or grated and added to a basic coleslaw — vegetables such as celeriac, fennel and baby turnip, along with soft herbs.

2 carrots, peeled and grated into long strips
400g red cabbage, trimmed and very finely sliced
400g white cabbage, trimmed and very finely sliced
3–4 leaves kale, very finely sliced (optional)
½ red onion, finely sliced
2 crunchy apples, very finely sliced
1 tablespoon chopped parsley
1 tablespoon chopped mint
250ml thick unsweetened yoghurt
1 tablespoon grainy mustard
1 tablespoon lemon juice or red wine vinegar
4 tablespoons extra virgin olive oil
salt and freshly ground black pepper

Combine all the vegetables, apple slices and herbs in a large bowl.

Whisk together the yoghurt, mustard, lemon juice and olive oil. Season to taste with salt and pepper.

Pour the dressing over the combined vegetables and toss well to coat. Place in a large bowl to serve.

Serves 6 as a side dish

CAULIFLOWER CHEESE

A family favourite using cheddar and buffalo mozzarella. Add some chopped parsley, chopped thyme leaves or some chopped capers to the cooked sauce if you wish. This can be eaten as a main course with a salad, or with thickly sliced ham.

1 medium-sized cauliflower, separated into florets (500g)
50g butter
3 tablespoons flour
3 cups milk (more if needed)
½ cup cream (more if needed)
1½ cups grated cheddar cheese
salt
250–300g buffalo mozzarella, coarsely torn
½ cup panko crumbs
extra ½ cup grated cheddar for topping

Preheat the oven to 200°C. Cook the cauliflower florets in plenty of lightly salted boiling water for four to five minutes, or until bite-tender. Drain well and set aside.

In a medium-sized saucepan, melt the butter over a low heat then stir in the flour to form a roux. Allow the roux to bubble gently, stirring continuously until lightly golden.

Add the milk and cream to the roux, about half a cup at a time. Whisk continuously, until all the milk and cream have been added and the sauce is thick enough to coat the back of a wooden spoon.

Stir in the grated cheddar and add salt to taste. Stir the cooked cauliflower through the cheese sauce, adding more cream or milk if you think the sauce is too thick.

Spoon into a lightly greased gratin dish or individual dishes and top with the mozzarella, panko crumbs and extra grated cheddar.

Place on an oven tray, then position this high in the oven. Cook until golden and bubbling, 10 to 15 minutes. Serve.

SERVES 4 AS A MAIN COURSE

FRIED CAULIFLOWER WITH TAHINI LEMON DRESSING

This very simple recipe is delicious. The cauliflower sweetens with frying and the exterior becomes crisp, while the tahini dressing provides a pleasing nutty note.

FOR THE TAHINI LEMON DRESSING
2 tablespoons tahini
1 lemon, juice
sea salt

FOR THE FRIED CAULIFLOWER
1 medium-sized cauliflower, cut into florets
2 tablespoons rice flour
½ teaspoon turmeric
oil for deep frying (we used rice bran oil)
salt

To make the dressing, mix together the tahini and lemon juice, then set aside. The mixture will stiffen and need to be diluted to a drizzling consistency with three to four tablespoons of water. Season to taste with salt.

To prepare the cauliflower, toss it with the rice flour and turmeric in a plastic bag, then shake off the excess dry ingredients.

Heat the oil to 180°C and fry the cauliflower in batches until golden, about four minutes.

Drain on paper towels, season with salt and serve immediately. Pass around the dressing for drizzling.

SERVES 6 AS A SIDE DISH

WHOLEWHEAT FUSILLI WITH CABBAGE AND POTATO

A peasant-style pasta dish that's great for winter when you are feeling particularly cold and hungry. Buttery cabbage and lots of melting cheese make this dish really comforting. Serve with a tasty chutney if you wish.

4 medium-sized potatoes, scrubbed
350g dried wholewheat fusilli pasta
500g green cabbage, trimmed and finely shredded
1 clove garlic, very finely sliced
100g butter
1 tablespoon chopped mint
½ tablespoon chopped thyme
freshly ground black pepper
300g good melting cheese (such as Fontina), thinly sliced
90g Parmigiano Reggiano, grated

Preheat the oven to 200°C. Boil the whole potatoes in salted water until just cooked, 25 to 30 minutes. Do not allow them to break up at this stage or they will become watery.

Meanwhile, cook the pasta in plenty of lightly salted water until al dente, about 10 minutes. Steam the cabbage with the garlic slices and half the butter until tender, about six minutes, then stir in the chopped mint and thyme.

Peel the cooked potatoes and cut into thin slices. Mix the two cheeses together. Grease a large gratin dish well with the remaining butter.

Place a layer of sliced potatoes in the base of the dish, then cover with half the pasta followed by half the cabbage. Season well with black pepper, then sprinkle half the cheese on top. Repeat the layering with the remaining potato, pasta, cabbage and cheese.

Place in the oven and cook for about 10 minutes, or until very hot and the cheese has melted.

If necessary, mix everything from top to bottom before serving, to ensure the cheese has melted all the way through. Serve immediately.

SERVES 6 AS A MAIN COURSE

Pasta With Cavolo Nero and Black Olive Sauce

Sometimes called Tuscan kale or black cabbage, cavolo nero is at its best after a good frost, when it becomes sweeter. Its central stem (best discarded, as it is rather coarse) has long leaves that are made tender by cooking. In Tuscany, cavolo nero is best enjoyed when the new season's peppery, pungent extra virgin olive oil is ready — if possible, use something similar for this recipe. Try a pasta such as rigatoncini, orecchiette or fusilli to catch the sauce.

500g cavolo nero
4 cloves garlic, peeled
100ml strong, peppery olive oil
2 small dried chillies, crumbled
3 tablespoons pitted black olives
400g dried pasta, such as rigatoncini, orecchiette or fusilli
50g Parmigiano Reggiano, grated

Strip the cavolo nero leaves from the stem (hold the stem with one hand and run your other hand down the sides to remove the leaves). Cook the leaves with the garlic in boiling salted water for 10 minutes or until the leaves are bite-tender.

Drain, reserving one cup of the cooking water. Set aside the garlic, and roughly chop the cavolo nero.

In a saucepan, heat two tablespoons of the olive oil, add the chilli and cavolo nero and sauté for a few minutes, until the garlic and chilli are fragrant and the cavolo nero is coated in the oil. Take half the cavolo nero and purée with the reserved garlic, the remaining olive oil and enough of the reserved blanching water to make a smooth purée. Return this to the saucepan with the olives.

Cook the pasta according to the packet instructions, until al dente. Meanwhile, warm bowls for serving.

Drain the pasta, then add it to the cavolo nero, stirring well to combine. Serve in the warmed bowls and pass around the grated Parmigiano Reggiano separately.

Serves 4 as a main course

Buttery Spiced Chokos

Chokos (also called chayote or mirliton) are often overlooked as, unadorned, they have very little flavour. However, cooked this way with curry powder, butter and parsley, the chokos are meltingly tender and surprisingly delicious. They will complement chicken or fish dishes.

4 large chokos, peeled
3–4 tablespoons butter
2 teaspoons curry powder
salt and freshly ground black pepper
3 tablespoons chopped parsley

Remove and discard the hard cores of the chokos. Cut the flesh into 8cm wedges.

In a heavy-based saucepan, melt the butter and add the curry powder. Allow the curry powder to sizzle gently in the butter, then add the choko wedges, tossing well.

Turn the heat very low and cook the chokos slowly until tender, turning occasionally. This should take eight to 10 minutes. If the chokos seem likely to catch, add a little water.

When tender, season to taste with salt and pepper, then toss in the chopped parsley. Serve hot.

Serves 4–6 as a side dish

Fennel and Bulghur Pilaf

Bulghur makes an excellent pilaf, but be sure to use a coarse type for this recipe.
For summer we replaced the fennel and leeks with courgettes and aubergines, adding
plenty of red chilli and mint.

2 tablespoons extra virgin olive oil
2 leeks, washed and cut into 2cm slices
2 bulbs fennel, cut into wedges,
  fronds reserved
½ cup coarse bulghur
1 tablespoon tomato paste
¾ cup stock (light vegetable or
  chicken) or water
½ lemon, juice
1 cup loosely packed Italian parsley,
  coarsely chopped
salt and freshly ground black pepper

In a large saucepan, heat the olive oil. Add the leeks and
fennel, and sauté gently for 10 minutes or until soft but
not coloured. Add the bulghur and cook for a minute.

Mix in the tomato paste and add the stock or water. Bring
to the boil, lower the heat to a gentle simmer, cover and
cook for 10 minutes.

Turn off the heat and leave, still covered, for 10 minutes.
Meanwhile, chop the reserved fennel fronds.

Remove the lid (the water should be absorbed) and toss
through the lemon juice, parsley and chopped fronds.
Season generously with salt and pepper.

Serves 4 as a side dish

Jerusalem Artichoke Soup

The Jerusalem artichoke is no relation to the globe artichoke, however some cooks find a similarity in taste. The knobbly little bodies of artichoke tubers are a fiddle to peel, displaying more curves than a beauty pageant, but peeling them is well worth the effort. They do need to be dropped into acidulated water immediately after peeling to stop them discolouring.

750g Jerusalem artichokes
  (peeled weight)
1 lemon, juice
50g butter
1 onion, peeled and finely sliced
600ml milk
600ml light vegetable stock or water
salt and freshly ground black pepper
30g (2 tablespoons) flour
150ml extra milk for blending
1 egg, beaten
150ml cream
croutons for serving

Peel an artichoke and drop immediately into water that has the juice of a lemon added. Repeat with the remaining artichokes, then slice and return them to the acidulated water.

Melt the butter in a large saucepan, add the sliced onion and cook until soft but not coloured. Add the sliced artichokes, then the first measure of milk. Cover the saucepan and shake over a low heat for about eight minutes.

Pour in the stock or water, season with salt and pepper, bring to the boil, then simmer for 15 to 20 minutes. Allow to cool a little, then place in a blender and reduce to a cream. Return the mixture to the saucepan.

In a bowl, blend the flour with the extra cold milk, strain into the pan and stir until boiling. Simmer for a few minutes.

Mix the beaten egg with the cream and add to the soup to enrich it. Serve with croutons.

SERVES 6–8 AS A STARTER

Kumara and Feta Fritters

Fritters are always a popular item on any menu. Serve these as small bite-sized fritters with a dollop of chutney to accompany drinks, or make them slightly larger and serve with poached eggs or smoked salmon for a light meal.

400g (2) medium-sized kumara, peeled
4–5 spring onions, finely chopped
3 tablespoons chopped thyme
3 eggs, beaten
salt and pepper
100g crumbly feta
8 tablespoons (120ml) light olive oil, more if needed

Grate the kumara and place in a sieve to allow any excess moisture to drain away.

In a large bowl combine the grated kumara with the spring onions and thyme. Mix well, adding the beaten egg and seasoning. Fold in the crumbled cheese gently.

Heat the oil in a heavy-based frying pan. When the oil is hot, drop in teaspoons (or tablespoons, for larger fritters) of the mixture and cook over a slow heat for two to three minutes, or until they are golden. Turn and cook the other side until golden. You will have to do these in batches and may need to replace the oil halfway through.

Place on paper towels to drain; keep warm. Serve bite-sized fritters topped with smoked salmon, a squeeze of lemon, a dab of crème fraîche and a sprig of thyme or chutney to accompany drinks, or larger fritters as part of a meal.

Makes 12–24 fritters

Chickpea and Leek Soup

This winter favourite is rich and hearty enough to serve as a meal on its own — and it has a beguiling sweetness, thanks to the leeks and rosemary. As with most simple Italian dishes, it builds flavour by slowly sweating the vegetables (called a soffrito). It's wonderfully nourishing for vegetarians and vegans. Be sure to use non-heat-treated chickpeas.

1 cup dried chickpeas
2 tablespoons olive oil
1 medium-sized onion, finely chopped
2 stalks celery, finely chopped
3 leeks, finely chopped
3 cloves garlic, finely chopped
1 tablespoon rosemary, very finely
   chopped
1½ litres stock (vegetable or chicken)
   or water
sea salt and freshly ground black
   pepper
1 bunch spinach leaves (stems
   removed), coarsely sliced
extra virgin olive oil for drizzling

Soak the chickpeas in water overnight. Drain just before using.

Heat the oil in a medium-sized saucepan. Sauté the onion, celery, leeks, garlic and rosemary very slowly, until soft but not coloured. This should take at least 30 minutes. (Don't be tempted to add salt at this stage to speed up the sweating of the vegetables; salt will toughen the chickpeas.)

Add the drained chickpeas and the stock or water, and bring to a gentle simmer. Cook until the chickpeas are tender (60 to 90 minutes), adding extra water if necessary.

Place two cups of the soup in a food processor and process until smooth. Add back to the soup, check for seasoning and add salt and pepper to taste. Just before serving, add the sliced spinach and cook until wilted.

Serve in bowls, drizzled with extra virgin olive oil.

Serves 6 as a main course

LEEK AND GOAT'S CHEESE TART

This delicious tart is perfect for a winter lunch. Serve with a salad of rocket leaves dressed with a sharp vinaigrette.

FOR THE SHORT PASTRY
240g standard flour
pinch salt
180g unsalted butter, chilled and diced
4 tablespoons chilled water

FOR THE FILLING
50g butter
2 large leeks (about 600g)
1 teaspoon chopped thyme leaves
¼ cup pitted olives
4 eggs
200g crème fraîche
salt and freshly ground black pepper
100g goat's cheese, crumbled

To make the pastry, place the flour and salt in a food processor. Pulse once to distribute the salt evenly, then add the butter and pulse until the mix resembles fine crumbs. Add the chilled water and pulse once or twice, but don't allow the mix to form a ball.

Turn out on a clean bench and knead lightly to bring together. Form into a ball and chill for at least two hours (the dough can also be frozen at this point, for use at a later date). On a lightly floured surface, roll out the dough to 4mm thick. Place into a 30cm tart tin and trim. Refrigerate for at least 30 minutes to rest. Meanwhile, preheat the oven to 180°C.

Prick the tart base with a fork, cover with baking paper and fill with dried beans, rice or ceramic beans. Blind-bake for 20 minutes. Remove the paper and beans, then cool the tart shell on a rack before filling.

To prepare the filling, first trim off and discard the green parts of the leeks. Thinly slice the white parts. Melt the butter in a large saucepan and add the leeks.

Sauté for five minutes, cover with a lid and steam for another five minutes, until the leeks are soft and uncoloured. Mix with the thyme and olives.

Lightly beat the eggs with the crème fraîche until smooth. Season with salt and pepper.

Place the leeks in the cooled tart shell, pour the egg mixture over them, then top with the crumbled goat's cheese.

Bake for 20 minutes or until the egg mixture has just set. Allow to cool for 10 minutes before cutting.

SERVES 6–8 AS A LUNCH DISH

SPICED LENTILS, TOMATO AND EGGS

This dish is quite hot, but you can easily tone it down by reducing the amount of harissa. You can also prepare the lentils ahead, then warm them up and add the eggs to finish. A delicious breakfast or lunch dish.

2 tablespoons olive oil
1 large onion, finely chopped
salt and freshly ground black pepper
4 cloves garlic, sliced
2 teaspoons ground coriander seeds
2 teaspoons ground cumin
1 tablespoon harissa (or to taste)
2 tomatoes, peeled and chopped
1 cup lentils (preferably Puy or
  Montebello)
2 preserved lemons (zest only),
  thinly sliced
1 cup chopped coriander leaves
3 cups stock or water
6 eggs
thick unsweetened yoghurt for
  garnishing

In a wide saucepan, heat the oil over a moderate heat, add the onion and salt and sauté gently until soft. Add the garlic, cook for a few minutes, then add the ground coriander and cumin, together with the harissa. Stir for a few minutes until fragrant.

Add the tomatoes and cook for five minutes, until broken down. Add the lentils, preserved lemons and half the coriander leaves. Pour in the stock or water, bring to the boil then gently simmer for 30 to 40 minutes, until most of the liquid has evaporated and the lentils are tender. Add a little more water during cooking if necessary. Check the seasoning and add extra salt if desired.

Press six small hollows evenly into the lentil mixture, crack in the eggs, then season with salt and pepper. Cover with a lid and cook over a moderate heat for five or six minutes, or until done to your liking.

Garnish with the remaining coriander leaves, extra harissa if desired and some yoghurt.

SERVES 6 FOR BREAKFAST OR AS A LUNCH DISH

Spiced Parsnip and Coconut Soup

A recipe inspired by English food writer Jane Grigson, whose favourite root vegetable soup was a curried parsnip soup. Here, shallots and parsnips are cooked in butter with a mixture of spices and well-flavoured vegetable or chicken stock. Thick coconut cream is added for a final touch.

2 tablespoons butter
5 medium shallots, finely chopped
1 teaspoon ground coriander seeds
1 teaspoon ground cumin
1 small dried red chilli
1 teaspoon turmeric
1 teaspoon ground cardamom
2 large parsnips, peeled and cut into
  small pieces
1 tablespoon flour
1 litre vegetable or chicken stock
200ml coconut cream
salt and freshly ground black pepper
small bunch chives, chopped

Melt the butter in a heavy saucepan and add the chopped shallots with all the spices. Cook over a low heat for five minutes, until the shallots are soft but not coloured.

Add the parsnips and continue to cook slowly, with a piece of baking paper pressed down on the surface and the saucepan lid on. When the parsnips have softened a little, after about 10 minutes, stir in the flour. Cook for a minute, then add the stock. Bring to a gentle simmer and cook for a further 20 minutes, stirring occasionally.

Cool slightly and purée in a food processor or blender until smooth. Strain and return the purée to the rinsed-out pan, add the coconut cream and season with salt and pepper to taste.

Reheat to serve, and garnish with a few chopped chives.

SERVES 6 AS A STARTER

Cumin Potatoes with Indian Chutney

Delicious finger food and a great stand-alone dish. Blanching the potato wedges before roasting will ensure a crisp wedge that is light and fluffy in the centre, though this step can be omitted. A good tip is to peel the ginger root with a teaspoon — it's quick and removes only the skin. The chutney keeps for up to five days in the refrigerator.

For the potato wedges

6 floury potatoes (such as Agria or
   Ilam Hardy)
4–6 tablespoons sunflower oil
1 tablespoon ground coriander seeds
2 teaspoons ground cumin
1 teaspoon salt
½ teaspoon freshly ground
   black pepper

For the Indian chutney

1 teaspoon mustard seeds
1 tablespoon sesame oil
1 clove garlic, crushed
½ teaspoon seeded and finely chopped
   red chilli
1 teaspoon grated ginger root
½ teaspoon ground cardamom
¼ teaspoon ground cinnamon
50g soft brown sugar
½ teaspoon salt
30g concentrated tamarind paste
400g can whole tomatoes in juice,
   roughly chopped

To prepare the potatoes, first preheat the oven to 190°C. Peel or scrub the potatoes and cut lengthwise into evenly sized wedges, 8 to 10cm long and 4cm thick.

Blanch the wedges for two to three minutes. Meanwhile, whisk together the oil, spices and seasoning.

Drain the potato wedges well and pat dry with paper towels. Place in a shallow roasting dish. Pour the oil mixture over the top and toss well to coat the potatoes.

Cook for 25 minutes until golden brown and cooked through. Shake the potatoes from time to time.

Meanwhile, prepare the chutney. Fry the mustard seeds in the sesame oil over a moderate heat for 30 seconds.

Remove from the heat and stir in the garlic, chilli, ginger, spices, sugar and salt. Cook over a low heat for about one minute, stirring constantly.

Add the tamarind and the tomatoes with their juice. Simmer over a low heat for 10 minutes until thick, stirring frequently.

Serve the potato wedges hot with a side bowl of Indian chutney.

Serves 6 for nibbles with drinks

Salad of Radicchio, Rocket, Oranges, Raisins and Pine Nuts

Radicchio is part of the bitter leaf clan and a few years ago it was part of every fashionable salad — until rocket came along. Here we have mixed the two together, but you could also add other leaves of your choice.

1 head radicchio, trimmed
6 large handfuls rocket, stems removed
3 oranges
1 tablespoon red wine vinegar
3 tablespoons extra virgin olive oil
¼ teaspoon salt
freshly ground black pepper
½ cup golden raisins
1 teaspoon extra virgin olive oil for pine nuts
½ cup pine nuts

Place the prepared radicchio and rocket in a large bowl and refrigerate.

Grate the zest of one orange. To segment all three oranges, use a serrated knife to cut a slice from the top of each orange, exposing the flesh. Cutting just beneath the pith, peel the orange over a bowl to collect the juice.

Cut each segment out from between the membrane divisions. The segments should be completely free of membrane and pith. Set aside.

Take the bowl with the collected juice and add the orange zest, vinegar, the first measure of olive oil, and salt and pepper. Whisk together. Add the raisins and let them marinate for a few minutes before removing and setting them aside.

Heat the remaining teaspoon of oil in a small frying pan and add the pine nuts. Using a wooden spoon, constantly move the pine nuts around the pan for two to three minutes or until golden.

Toss the salad leaves with the orange vinaigrette. Divide between six serving plates and top with the orange segments, raisins and pine nuts; alternatively, place everything in a salad bowl. Serve immediately.

Serves 6 as a starter

WINTER RICE SALAD

Rice plays a minor rather than dominating part in this tasty dish. It can be prepared a day ahead (allowing the diverse flavours to meld), refrigerated and then returned to room temperature before serving. Perfect for a crowd.

1 cup basmati rice
2 tablespoons olive oil
1 small onion, finely chopped
2 cloves garlic, crushed
3 cups chicken stock
2 red peppers
½ cup unsweetened yoghurt
1 lemon, juice and finely grated zest
½ teaspoon salt
1 teaspoon freshly ground black pepper
½ teaspoon dried red chilli flakes
500g spinach, stems discarded
1 cup frozen peas, cooked and drained
2 quarters preserved lemon (zest only),
   finely diced
1 large bunch Italian parsley, leaves
   finely chopped
8 sprigs mint, leaves finely sliced

Wash the rice well, and leave to soak in cold water for 30 minutes. Preheat the oven to 180°C.

Heat the olive oil in a heavy-based saucepan, add the onion and garlic and cook over a very gentle heat until softened and golden. Add the rice, toss for a minute or two over the heat, turn the heat up and pour in the stock.

Bring to a simmer, cover with the lid, lower the heat and allow to cook until the rice is soft and all the liquid is absorbed. This should take 12 to 15 minutes. Remove from the heat, stir with a fork and cool a little.

Meanwhile, prepare the peppers. Place them in an oven dish and roast for about 20 minutes, until the skins are blistered and turning black. Take them from the oven and put them in a bag so the skins loosen. Remove and discard the skins, stems and seeds and cut the flesh into thin strips.

Make a dressing for the rice by mixing the yoghurt, lemon juice and zest, salt and pepper and chilli flakes. Toss the still warm rice in this mixture.

Shred the spinach or cut into very fine slices. Transfer the dressed rice to a large serving bowl, then add the peppers, peas, spinach, preserved lemon and herbs. Toss well together with two large forks (this will prevent the rice from clumping together).

Taste for seasoning and adjust if necessary. Serve at room temperature.

SERVES 8–10 AS A SIDE DISH

CREAMED SPINACH

This classic dish is a grand accompaniment to grilled meats or poached salmon. It can be even finer by adding pitted olives and finishing with a grating of Parmigiano Reggiano.

1 large bunch spinach (around 200g),
  stems discarded
25g butter
2 cloves garlic, finely chopped
100ml cream
a good grating of nutmeg
salt and freshly ground black pepper

Blanch the spinach in boiling salted water until it has wilted (one to two minutes), then drain. When cool enough to handle, squeeze out the excess moisture (either use your hands to squeeze small handfuls of spinach or wrap it all in a clean tea towel and twist out the moisture). Finely chop the spinach and set aside.

Melt the butter in a medium-sized saucepan, add the garlic and sauté gently for a minute. Add the spinach and make sure it is well coated. Add the cream and cook for a further minute.

Grate nutmeg over the creamed mixture and season well with salt and pepper. Serve immediately.

SERVES 4 AS A SIDE DISH

Roasted Yams with Spiced Butter

Yams with this spiced butter are a great accompaniment to roast lamb in the winter. Roast the yams until they still have a little crunch to them.

500g yams, washed and dried
1 tablespoon oil
salt and freshly ground black pepper
60–70g butter, softened
1½ teaspoons ground cumin
¼ preserved lemon (rind only),
    finely diced
juice of ½ lemon

Preheat the oven to 190°C. Place the yams in a shallow roasting dish, pour the oil over them and toss to coat. Season with salt and pepper.

Roast for about 20 minutes, shaking the roasting dish from time to time during the cooking.

Place the butter in a small bowl and blend in the cumin, preserved lemon and lemon juice.

Place the hot yams in a serving bowl, dotting the spiced butter over to melt. Serve immediately.

SERVES 4 AS A SIDE DISH

BRAISED BABY TURNIPS WITH THYME AND HONEY

Many people find turnips too bitter — usually because they haven't removed enough of the skin. Baby turnips are usually fairly sweet but we peel them just in case. Any attached green leaves are delicious blanched then added to the braised turnips just before serving. Ordinary turnips can be used: chop them into large chunks before using.

1 tablespoon olive oil
25g butter
500g baby turnips, trimmed and peeled
2 cloves garlic, peeled and halved
1 sprig thyme, leaves only
1 cup vegetable or chicken stock
1 tablespoon liquid honey
salt and freshly ground black pepper

Put the oil and butter in a small saucepan and heat until the butter starts to foam. Add the turnips and coat in the butter for a few minutes to colour lightly. Add the garlic and thyme, stir for a minute then add the stock.

Bring to the boil, cover and cook over a gentle heat for 15 minutes or until the turnips are cooked. Meanwhile, heat a serving bowl. Drain and discard the stock.

Drizzle the honey on top of the turnips, season with salt and pepper to taste and toss gently to combine. Transfer to the heated bowl and serve immediately.

SERVES 4 AS A SIDE DISH

VEGETABLE STOCK

Making your own vegetable stock is simple and inexpensive. You know what you are putting into it, and what to expect once it's cooked. Vegetable stock often has a neutral taste, but caramelising the onion first (before adding the other ingredients) will help maximise the extraction of the natural sugars, resulting in more flavour. Pressing hard on the vegetables after straining also extracts maximum flavour.

100ml olive oil
3 large onions, chopped
1 large leek, sliced
3 carrots, sliced
3 celery stalks, sliced
2 large very ripe tomatoes,
    roughly chopped
100g mushroom trimmings
few fennel trimmings, optional
6 cloves garlic, roughly chopped
6 black peppercorns
1 bay leaf
few parsley stems
2 large sprigs thyme
4 litres cold water

Heat the olive oil over a low heat in a stockpot, add the onions and cook for about 20 minutes, stirring regularly, until they are caramelised.

Add all the remaining vegetables and aromatics to the stockpot with the water. Bring to the boil, then reduce to simmering point and simmer for three hours.

Allow to cool before pushing firmly through a finely meshed strainer. Refrigerate for up to two days, or freeze until needed.

MAKES ABOUT 3 LITRES

Roast Root Vegetables

These are a delight, and a favourite accompaniment for a roast or grilled meal.
By parboiling the potatoes and kumara before they go in the oven, you will have really
crispy roasted veggies. This is a dish that cannot be cooked in advance but you can
prepare the vegetables, including doing the parboiling, ahead of time.

4 large roasting potatoes (Agria
  or similar)
4 large kumara
salt and freshly ground black pepper
1kg pumpkin, peeled and seeded
4 thick parsnips, peeled
4 tablespoons olive oil
handful thyme sprigs

Preheat the oven to 200°C and place a large shallow
roasting pan in the oven to heat.

Peel the potatoes and kumara and cut into even pieces.
Place in a large saucepan, cover with water, add
1 tablespoon salt and bring to the boil. Simmer for about
10 minutes, and drain well.

Cut the pumpkin into chunks about the same size as the
kumara and potatoes. Cut the parsnips into long slices,
lengthwise.

Add the olive oil to the heated pan, tip all the vegetables in
and toss to coat lightly in oil. Grind pepper over the top,
add salt and thyme, and cook until crisp and golden, about
50 minutes. Heat a serving platter, transfer the vegetables
to it and serve at once.

Serves 8 as a side dish

HEARTY WINTER VEGETABLE SOUP

Here's a meal that is a true vegetarian treat. The base for this soup is the wonderful bounty of the cold months; a variety of root vegetables, leeks and onions combined with orzo pasta. The rice-like pasta is perfect as each piece is tiny and fits perfectly in a spoonful of chunky soup like this. Add a few lightly blanched green vegetables and herbs just before serving to enliven and freshen the soup. Any leftovers will refrigerate well to serve the following day.

8 tablespoons (120ml) avocado oil
1 onion, finely chopped
2 leeks, finely sliced
2 medium-sized potatoes, peeled
    and diced
250g pumpkin, peeled and diced
2 kumara, peeled and diced
2 carrots, peeled and diced
1 teaspoon sweet paprika
4 sprigs thyme
400g can whole tomatoes in juice
1 litre vegetable stock
½ cup orzo
salt and freshly ground black pepper
200g green beans, trimmed
½ cup green peas (frozen are fine)
4–5 leaves silver beet, stems removed
    and leaves shredded
½ cup Italian parsley leaves

Heat half the avocado oil in a saucepan, and add the onion and leeks. Cook for about eight minutes over very gentle heat, until the onion is translucent and soft.

Add the potato, pumpkin, kumara and carrot dice with the paprika and thyme sprigs. Stir and continue to cook gently for five minutes.

Mash the tomatoes and juice together, then add to the pan with the vegetable stock and orzo pasta. Bring to a simmer and allow to bubble away for 10 minutes. Check for seasoning, adding salt and pepper to taste.

Meanwhile, blanch the beans, peas and silver beet in salted boiling water for two minutes, and refresh under cold water.

When ready to serve, add the green vegetables with the parsley, return to a simmer for three minutes before ladling out into bowls and finishing each serving with a drizzle of avocado oil. Serve with fresh wholegrain bread.

SERVES 10 AS A MAIN

Cajun Vegetable Stew

Don't let the number of ingredients put you off — this is delicious. Serve as a meal in itself with fresh bread, or with pan-fried chicken.

2 tablespoons oil
3 onions, cut into 2.5cm dice
1–2 tablespoons chopped garlic
2 tablespoons coriander seeds, ground
½ teaspoon grated nutmeg
½ teaspoon allspice, ground
1 teaspoon cumin, ground
2 cups peeled and diced pumpkin
  (1.5cm dice)
1 cup peeled and diced kumara
  (1.5cm dice)
1 red pepper, seeded and cut into
  1.5cm dice
1–2 red chillies, seeded and finely
  chopped
400g can whole tomatoes in juice,
  roughly chopped
400ml coconut cream
425g can whole-kernel corn, drained
2 sprigs oregano
2 sprigs thyme
½ cup orange juice
salt
1 tablespoon chopped coriander leaves

Heat the oil in a large heavy-based pan with a lid. Cook the onions until soft, about five minutes. Add the garlic, ground coriander, nutmeg, allspice and cumin and cook for 30 seconds.

Add the pumpkin, kumara, pepper and chillies and toss, coating the vegetables in the spices. Add the tomatoes and juice, coconut cream, corn, fresh herbs and orange juice. Season with salt.

Cover and simmer on a very low heat for 50 to 60 minutes, until the vegetables are tender. They should still be whole pieces rather than mushy.

Stir the chopped coriander through the stew and serve hot.

SERVES 8–10 AS A MAIN

ABOUT THE AUTHORS

LAURAINE JACOBS

Lauraine Jacobs is passionate about artisan produce, farmers' markets, wine and fresh, healthy food. Well respected worldwide for her knowledge of food, wine and restaurant trends, she has authored eight cookbooks, including *The Confident Cook* and *Matakana*, both published by Random House. She is a former president of the US-based International Association of Culinary Professionals, was a member of the New Zealand Government Food & Beverage Taskforce 2006/2007 and currently serves as president of the New Zealand Guild of Food Writers. She has written for *Fashion Quarterly*, *Cuisine*, *Cuisine Wine Country* and numerous international publications. Lauraine was made a Member of the New Zealand Order of Merit in the 2009 Queen's Birthday honours. She resides in Auckland, New Zealand. Her website is www.laurainejacobs.co.nz

GINNY GRANT

Ginny Grant is a deputy food editor at award-winning *Cuisine* magazine and a freelance food stylist. Her inspiration comes from the foods of the Mediterranean, with a particular love of the regional cuisines of Italy. She likes to cook simple food, prepared with a minimum of fuss using the freshest produce available. Ginny's background is in the hospitality industry, cooking in a diverse range of restaurants and cafes from the River Café in London to Boulcott St Bistro and Nikau Gallery Café in Wellington, and Delicious in Auckland. She resides in Auckland with her partner Daniel and their two young sons.

KATHY PATERSON

Kathy Paterson taught cooking at the Cordon Bleu Cookery School in London and returned to New Zealand to teach at the Cordon Bleu, Parnell, Auckland. She then spent 20 years running a highly successful, exclusive Auckland catering company, through which she arranged events from small dinner parties to society weddings. After selling her business, Kathy worked at Villa Maria Wines helping to set up their events centre at Mangere. Kathy is a regular contributor to *Real* magazine and private chef to Auckland-based businessman Craig Heatley and his family, through which she satisfies her need to keep 'hands-on cooking'. This is Kathy's second cookbook. She resides in Auckland and spends as much time as she can on the family farm in the Wairarapa.

From left: Kathy Paterson, Lauraine Jacobs and Ginny Grant

BIBLIOGRAPHY

Alexander, Stephanie, *The Cook's Companion*, Lantern, 2004

Bareham, Lindsey, *The Big Red Book of Tomatoes*, Penguin, 2000

Barron, Rosemary, *Meze*, Chronicle Books, 2002

Beck, Simone, Bertholle, Louise, Child, Julia, *Mastering the Art of French Cooking*, Penguin, 1966

Browne, Mary, Leach Helen, Tichborne, Nancy, *The Cook's Garden*, A.H.& A.W Reed, 1980

Carluccio, Antonio, *Vegetables*, Headline, 2000

Gourley, Glenda, *Vegetables A User's Guide*, Horticulture New Zealand, 2007

Gray, Rose, Rogers, Ruth, *The River Café Cook Book*, Ebury, 1995

————, *River Café Cook Book Green*, Ebury, 2000

Grigson, Jane, *Jane Grigson's Vegetable Book*, Penguin, 1980

Jacobs, Lauraine, *Matakana*, Random House, 2008

————, *The Confident Cook*, Random House, 2006

La Place, Viana, *Verdura*, Macmillan 1994

Little, Alastair, *Keep It Simple*, Conran Octopus, 1993

Madison, Deborah, *Local Flavours*, Broadway Books, 2002

————, *The Savory Way*, Bantam, 1990

Roden, Claudia, *The Book of Jewish Food*, Penguin, 1996

Schneider, Elizabeth, *Vegetables from Amaranth to Zucchini*, William Morrow, 2001

Shaida, Margaret, *The Legendary Cuisine of Persia*, Interlink, 2002

Waters, Alice, *Chez Panisse Vegetables*, Harper Collins, 1996

Weir, Joanne, *From Tapas to Meze*, Crown, 1994

Wells, Patricia, *Bistro Cooking*, Workman, 1989

ACKNOWLEDGEMENTS

We are indebted to chefs we have worked with, and to the many food writers around the world who inspire our work. We can't possibly list everyone but we particularly love, and return to, the writings and wisdom of Alice Waters, Antonio Carluccio, Claudia Roden, Deborah Madison, Elizabeth David, Jane Grigson, Joanne Weir, Marcella Hazan, Patricia Wells, Raymond Blanc, Rosemary Barron, Sam and Sam Clark, Stephanie Alexander and Ruth Rogers and the late Rose Gray.

We are very appreciative of the involvement of photographer Aaron McLean and for his fine eye for detail. He is always a delight to work with, even if he did think that working with three cooks was 'like an extreme sport'. And our thanks to our stylist Tam West, who has an innate sense of exactly what is required to make our work look great.

The team at Random House are great to work with, and we've loved working with Nicola Legat, Sarah Ell and Alex Bishop. We're also delighted with the clean and clear design and layout that Keely O'Shannessy has given this book. And thanks to the very patient and talented Claire Gummer, who tirelessly worked through editing our words and who ensured our recipes are achievable for everyone.

We'd also like to thank our respective parents and families for their loyal support and for instilling in each of us a love of good food and wine. And to Murray and Daniel, many thanks for your companionship and ongoing encouragement.

And finally we're grateful to the unsung heroes of vegetable production — the growers and farmers who toil long hours to bring us terrific produce to cook and eat. We love your veges and hope that more cooks will be inspired to get into the kitchen and cook their way to better health.

INDEX

A RANDOM HOUSE BOOK published by Random House New Zealand
18 Poland Road, Glenfield, Auckland, New Zealand

For more information about our titles go to www.randomhouse.co.nz

A catalogue record for this book is available from the National Library of New Zealand

Random House New Zealand is part of the Random House Group
New York   London   Sydney   Auckland   Delhi   Johannesburg

First published 2010. Reprinted 2012.

© 2010 recipes Ginny Grant, Kathy Paterson, Lauraine Jacobs; photographs Aaron McLean

The moral rights of the authors have been asserted

ISBN 978 1 86979 365 4

Photography by Aaron McLean
Styling: Tam West
Design: Keely O'Shannessy
Printed in China by Bookbuilders